The Empty God

Other Works by Al Hill

Our Evil—God's Good
And Other Sermons from Genesis through Joshua

Things That Kings Can't Do
And Other Sermons from Judges through 2nd Kings, and the Wisdom Books

In the Presence of the Lord
And Other Sermons from the Psalms and the Prophets

Walking with Jesus
And Other Sermons from the Gospel of Matthew

God's Purpose for Your Faith
And Other Sermons from the Gospel of Mark, Hebrews, James and 1st Peter

From Jerusalem to Jericho
And Other Sermons from the Gospel of Luke and the Acts of the Apostles

Traits of the Shepherd
And Other Sermons from the Gospel of John, 1st John and Revelation

Making Peace with Your Father
And Other Sermons from Paul's Letters to the Romans and Corinthians

O Come, Let God Adore Us
And Other Sermons for Advent and Christmas

Not Exactly What They Expected
And Other Sermons for Holy Week and Easter

DEAR TRINITY
Letters from a Pastor to His People

The Empty God

*And Other Sermons
from the Shorter Letters of Paul*

Al Hill

SOMMERTON
HOUSE

Because of the dynamic nature of the Internet, any web addresses or links contained in this book may have changed since publication and may no longer be valid.

Cover design by the author.

The image on the cover—"Jesus Taken Down from the Cross"—is from a stained-glass window created by F. X. Zettler in 1911. The window is located in the Buffalo Religious Arts Center (https://www.buffaloreligiousarts.org/) (formerly St. Francis Xavier Catholic Church), in Buffalo, New York. The image is used with the gracious permission of the Center and with great appreciation to Mrs. Mary Holland, who went "above and beyond the call of duty"—literally—to provide the photograph reproduced here.

ISBN: 978-1-948773-17-1 (sc)

Library of Congress Control Number: 2018904867

To learn more about or purchase this or other works by Al Hill, go to www.sommertonhouse.com, or www.amazon.com/author/alhill.

Dedication

To the memory of Annie and Claude Stanfield,
my "Maamaw" and "Grandaddy."

The former taught me to read
before I was old enough to go to school,
and launched a life-long love of language
that has blessed me beyond measure.

The latter was my first great friend and hero,
whose untimely death, early in my life,
I grieve to this day.

Contents

Sermons

Indices

Preface

Throughout the ministry of Jesus, He instructed His disciples in what it meant to be disciples. Jesus came to call men and women to repentance and faith. The result of such a response was God-given reconciliation—with God, first of all—and then, with "neighbors"—as Jesus defined them.

The divine message Jesus conveyed came out of the law and history of their shared Jewish heritage—but not self-evidently so. The gospel was the gospel (good news) because of the unfamiliar way that Jesus put the familiar pieces together. Even with His help, His disciples continued to have a hard time putting the pieces together to see the picture Jesus was painting for them. After His Resurrection—and with His help and that of the Holy Spirit later—they began to see things more clearly.

When the gospel expanded beyond Judaism, it became necessary to explain the good news to people who did not know what the Jews knew about the nature and activity of their God across centuries of history. In their letters, Peter, James, John and (especially) Paul, led new believers on a quest of understanding and appreciation of what God had done—and was continuing to do—in Jesus Christ.

Much of the Christian gospel turned out to be "counter-intuitive" to the prevailing thought patterns of the world. Even in the Gospels, Jesus pointed out that *"the last will be first and the first last,*"[1] and that to be greatest of all required becoming the servant of all.[2]

Paul picks up that idea when he points out that God's *"power is made perfect in weakness."*[3] And Paul takes the idea even deeper spiritually when he writes about the extent of the sacrifice God made for our salvation: God completely emptied Himself of His divine powers to be able to do what any form of power (as we understand it) would have prevented Him from doing.[4]

In these shorter letters of Paul (Galatians, Ephesians, Philippians, Colossians, 1st Thessalonians, and 1st and 2nd Timothy), the Apostle explores that mystery—and many of the other most important aspects of God's saving grace—and the nature of the relationship God has established with us, and for us, in the Church. And the more we know about what the gospel is, the deeper its impact on us—and the closer we grow in faith and fellowship with this God Who became a Man to save us.

৵৽

Most of the sermons in this collection were drawn from texts that appeared in the Revised Common Lectionary, and so the same texts "came up" every third year. For that reason, several sermons "share" the same passage of scripture.[5]

"The 'Submission Thing'" and "And Now: The Husbands" are a different category. They were "bookend" sermons, preached on successive Sundays in "the spirit of fair play."

The Lectionary always pairs an Epistle reading with a Gospel passage (and one or two others from the Old Testament). However, only sermons that drew significantly from the Epistle

---

[1] Matthew 20:16, RSV.
[2] Matthew 23:11.
[3] 2 Corinthians 12:9, ESV.
[4] See Philippians 2:5-8.
[5] Specifically: "The Fruit of Freedom" and "Free to Bear Good Fruit"; "Seeing with Your Heart" and "Far Above All"; "Off the Same Sheet of Music," "The Empty God" and "Imagine a Light"; and "That I May" and "Total Loss—Greater Gain."

readings are included in this collection. When a second reading also figured in the content of the sermon, that text is provided before the sermon as well. There were several years when I did not follow the Lectionary, and so there are sermons in the book whose texts are not found in the Lectionary.

Each sermon in this collection was written in full manuscript before it was preached, but all were written to be preached—to be heard, by a group of people, in church, during worship. Your reading will, of course, lack the benefit of vocal inflection, eye contact, body language, gestures and the "group dynamic."

On the other hand, you will have benefits the original audience lacked: You may pause whenever and wherever you wish—and re-read any or all of a sermon as many times as you want. You can choose which sermon you will "receive," rather than being stuck with whatever one I chose to deliver on any given day.

As you read, you will find the texts of different sermons rendered in different versions of the Bible. The sermons were preached in various Navy chapels and civilian churches over a number of years, and I generally used the particular translation of the "pew Bibles" where I was preaching at the time. One translation I used frequently is no longer available for publication, and I have substituted the English Standard Version for it throughout the book.

In preparing this and the other 10 volumes in the series for publication, I have added footnotes that were not part of the original oral presentations. When I am quoting scripture *verbatim*, the version is included in the footnote. When I paraphrase something in the Bible, or merely allude to it, only the reference is provided. Many footnotes have been provided to indicate the location of the scriptural authority for something I am asserting.

These references are organized in biblical order in an index in the back of the book. I have also provided an alphabetized list of the sermon titles, a sequential list of sermons texts, a list of texts that are included in the Revised Common Lectionary, and a summary of where, in other volumes, these and other sermons from Paul's shorter epistles may be found. I hope you will find these additions useful; I was always pleased to find such tools in books I used for study or devotion.

My practice has been to capitalize nouns and pronouns that refer to the Father, Son or Holy Spirit—even though the modern literary convention is to not do so. My small act of reverence may serve you by providing added clarity. The exception to this practice is with copyrighted material, where I reproduce the scripture as published in the versions I have used.

I have compiled this and its companion volumes primarily for those who continue to prepare sermons each week. I often read the sermons of other preachers as part of my own preparation, and I was always grateful to be able to follow someone else's thought process and discover some idea or turn of phrase that might ignite a whole new line of inquiry or inspiration.

Of course, sermons are for "everybody," and I hope that whoever you are, you will find something in the pages of this book that will draw you closer to Christ and enrich your understanding of the faith we share.

శ~ళ

Sermons

From the Letter to the Galatians

1.

The Son of God and You

Galatians 2:20 RSV

I have been crucified with Christ; it is no longer I who live, but Christ who lives in me; and the life I now live in the flesh I live by faith in the Son of God, who loved me and gave himself for me.

৯৯

For the past year and a half, I have had the honor and privilege to stand in this place and talk to you about the most important thing in the world: the good news of God's salvation in Jesus Christ and what that means for your life and mine. You have been kind enough to hear me, and today, I will impose upon your patience one last time.[6]

In recent days, in the aftermath of the national election,[7] many of those who were shocked and dismayed by the outcome pointed with alarm to the part they believe Christians played in the result. Remarkable accusations have been leveled at those who apparently take their relationship to Christ so seriously and identify

---

[6] This was my final sermon as Command Chaplain at the Little Creek (Virginia) Navy Chapel before being transferred (well ahead of my normal rotation date) to meet a need that had developed elsewhere.

[7] This sermon was preached in November 2004.

themselves with Christianity so closely that they actually allowed their religious convictions to affect—and perhaps even determine—their choice of candidates and positions on ballot initiatives.

"This is dangerous," people say. "This is radical," they assert. They are certain that any involvement of Christianity in the political life of this country is a profound problem.

☙❧

I do not share their concern. Nor, I believe, does the Founder of Christianity.

But there is a profound problem associated with Christianity. It's not the over-involvement of Christianity in the political life of this country. The problem is the inadequate involvement of Christianity in the personal lives of individuals—in this country, and every other country around the world.

Please note that I said, *"inadequate involvement,"* not *"lack* of involvement," for Christianity is involved in every person's life, because Christ is involved in every person's life, whether that person is a Christian or not. Christ is involved in *your* life, whether *you* are a Christian or not.

Let me show you how.

The Apostle Paul draws it out pretty well in the verse you just heard: Galatians 2:20. Paul is in the middle of an argument (that we won't worry about right now) as he writes this particular verse.

Paul is describing his own experience with Christ, but in several significant ways he is describing the involvement of Jesus Christ in the life of every man, woman, boy and girl who ever drew a breath on this earth. Here is the involvement of Christ in your life—to one degree or another.

Paul says, *"the Son of God...loved me..."*

"Well, of course," you may be thinking. "Jesus *would* love Paul. Paul is probably the greatest Christian who ever lived! Paul took the story of Jesus and spread it across the world. He founded churches and wrote a big chunk of the New Testament."

But Paul doesn't say, *"the Son of God **loves** me"* (present tense). Paul says, *"the Son of God **loved** me"* (past tense).

Does the grammar matter?

Yes. It matters.

Paul is saying that the Son of God loved who he was when who he was was *not* the greatest Christian who ever lived—or anything like it. Christ loved Paul when Paul was His publicly declared—and very active—enemy.

Before Paul even heard of Jesus, Jesus loved him. Before Paul decided to track down and persecute the followers of Jesus, Jesus had already chosen to love Paul—to strike him down on the Damascus Road and blind him[8]—and love him.

And when Paul says that the Son of God loved him, he's not saying anything that isn't true of every human being on earth. The Son of God loved Paul. The Son of God loved everybody. That's why our Bible says, *"For God so loved the world that he gave his only begotten Son..."*[9] and why Jesus says, *"I and the Father are one."*[10] And if true for everyone, then also true for you: The Son of God loved you.

Before you ever did anything bad in your life, the Son of God loved you. While you were doing bad things, the Son of God loved you.

And now that you have done bad things—and will do more— the Son of God who loved you still loves you. Think of the greatest love you ever heard about—the greatest love you've ever known or felt—the greatest love you can imagine. The greatest love you can think of is still a faint, faint shadow of the love the Son of God loved you with from the beginning of Creation and loves you with now.

---

[8] Acts 9:3-9.
[9] John 3:16, RSV.
[10] John 10:30, RSV.

Having trouble with your "love life"? The Son of God loves you. Say this to yourself: "The Son of God loved me." Meditate on that reality for a moment.

The Son of God loved Paul and He loved you and loved you still, and there is nothing you can do that can stop that love for you. You can separate yourself from the love of God, if you choose to reject it, but you cannot stop it. Ray Charles may have sung, "I can't stop loving you"[11] a thousand times, but he could have—and may have—stopped loving any number of people. But for God the Father and His beloved Son, these words are absolutely true: It is in the very nature of God in Christ to love you,[12] and He will never stop loving you—ever.[13]

Whoever you are, Christ has chosen to involve Himself in your life—by loving you.

And, according to Paul, the Son of God who loved Paul also *"gave himself up"* for Paul. And again, what the Son of God did for Paul, He did for every man, woman and child on earth—including you. You didn't even have to ask the Son of God to do it for you.[14] You couldn't have paid Him to do it—not in a million years—even if He would have let you, which He wouldn't.

As wonderful as it is to know that you are loved by the Son of God, that's how stunning and humbling it is to know that He also gave Himself up for you. He gave Himself up as an offering,[15] a sacrifice,[16] a payment in full for the penalty[17] you could not begin to satisfy.

We honor the young men and women who are giving themselves up for us every day in Afghanistan and Iraq. They give

---

[11] "I Can't Stop Loving You," was written by country singer and song writer Don Gibson in 1957 and recorded by Ray Charles in 1962.
[12] 1 John 4:8-9.
[13] Lamentations 3:22.
[14] Romans 5:8.
[15] Ephesians 5:2.
[16] Hebrews 10:12.
[17] Colossians 2:14.

themselves up to make it harder for a bunch of mad murderers to murder you and me and everyone else in what we think of as the civilized, peace-loving world. You here, more than most, understand what it means to give yourself or someone you love up for others. You understand what they are doing. You understand that they are doing it for you.

Do you understand why the Son of God gave Himself up for you? Do you understand that Jesus gave Himself up to the torturers so that you would not be tortured because of your sins? Do you understand that Jesus gave Himself up to the judgment of men so that you would not be given up in your sin to the judgment of God? Do you understand that Jesus gave Himself up to death so that you might live?

Centuries before the birth of Jesus, an Old Testament prophet wrote of a Suffering Servant who *"poured out his soul to death...[who] bore the sins of many, and made intercession for the transgressors."*[18] The Son of God loved you and gave Himself up for you. The Son of God loved and gave Himself up for everyone. And to that degree, the involvement of Christ in the life of every individual, saint or sinner, saved or lost, Christian or non-believer, is the same.

࿔

This involvement is incredible, miraculous—and ultimately inadequate. It is not enough.

As wonderful as it is that the Son of God loved you and gave Himself up for you, whoever you are, you are no better off than if none of this were true, if that is all you can say. He loved and gave Himself up for everybody, but most people are still going to hell.

What's the missing piece?

Let's go back to Galatians. Paul says three things about Christ's relationship with him in the verse we read. We've looked at two of them. But, in this case, "two out of three" *is* bad. In this case, it has

---

[18] Isaiah 53:12, RSV.

to be "all or nothing." Paul says the Son of God loved him—and gave Himself up for him—and that Christ, the Son of God, lives in him.

The difference for the Christian—the reason that the involvement of Christ in the life of a Christian is sufficient is that Christ lives within the Christian—within *you*, if you are a Christian. Christ does not live within the non-Christian. Christ does not live in the non-Christian even though God has made all the preparations necessary for that to happen. God has made all the preparations necessary for Christ to live in everyone.

It did not require anything from you for the Son of God to love you, or to give Himself up for you. But for Christ to live *in* you—*you* have to get involved with Christ. Paul talks in this verse about three ways he got involved with the Christ who loved Him and gave Himself up for him.

Paul says, *"I have been crucified with Christ."* This was Paul's response when he finally realized the truth of what we've been talking about: Christ's love and sacrifice for him. Paul judged himself by God's standard and admitted his guilt that deserved the punishment Jesus endured for him. Paul "personalized" the Crucifixion. Jesus' Crucifixion became Paul's Crucifixion: the Crucifixion of Jesus *for Paul*.

And in order for you to become a Christian, to have Christ live in you, you must do as Paul has done and make the Crucifixion of Jesus your own. You must nail your life of sin to that Cross where Jesus hangs so that it will die with Him. The Son of God loved me and gave Himself up for me and I give my pitiful life of sin over to Him so that He can do away with it. Paul says, *"It is no longer I who live."* He gave up his belief that his life was "all right." He recognized that it was so permeated with sin that it had to be exterminated on the Cross of Christ. But he also recognized that that wasn't enough if he was to become a Christian—if Christ was to be allowed to fulfill the goal of His love and the purpose of His sacrifice.

Paul also had to give up control of whatever he had left after his sinful life was crucified with Christ. If I may borrow a term much used and abused of late: Paul recognized the need for and submitted to a "regime change" in his life. *"It is no longer I who live, but Christ who lives in me."*

Who's your Savior? The One you are crucified with. Who's your Lord? The One Who lives in you and calls the shots in your life. And if Christ lives in you, how do you live? Paul says, *"The life I now live...I live by faith in the Son of God."*

What do they say about Christianity?

Dangerous?

Radical?

They're absolutely right. To *"live by faith in the Son of God who loved [you] and gave himself up for [you]"* is certainly going to seem radical to those who are obsessed with getting ahead in this world. To live *"by faith in the Son of God"* is definitely dangerous to those who've bet everything in the world on this world being all there is to bet on.

How sad—how tragic—to be two-thirds of the way to the kingdom of God and never enter in to glory! To have the Son of God love you and die for you, and yet not to let Him live in you, would seem like the ultimate waste —when all you have to do is give Him your life of sin, and submit to His authority in your life, and trust Him for everything else.

But that's the problem with Christianity: inadequate involvement. Please don't let it be your problem. Christianity can only be so involved, unless you respond to the Son of God. Love and sacrifice are not enough, even when they are Christ's. To be a Christian, you must let Him be fully involved. You must let Christ live in you.

Won't you let Him...live in you?

❧❦

Galatians 4:4-7 NRSV

[4] *But when the fullness of time had come, God sent his Son, born of a woman, born under the law,* [5] *in order to redeem those who were under the law, so that we might receive adoption as children.* [6] *And because you are children, God has sent the Spirit of his Son into our hearts, crying, "Abba! Father!"* [7] *So you are no longer a slave but a child, and if a child then also an heir, through God.*

಄⸙

2.

What Did You Get for Christmas?

Galatians 4:4-7 NRSV

Well, here we are—the Sunday after Christmas. I don't know the liturgical calendar well enough to know if today has a special title or designation. We could just call it "Exhaustion Sunday."

If you didn't wear yourself out cooking or baking, you probably outdid yourself eating the culinary contributions of others. Wonderful family gatherings (as wonderful as they are) can generate an awful lot of wear and tear on the body and the emotions, whether you're hosting, or traveling, or waiting for the weather to let you travel to where you can be hosted.

And then there's the business of presents. If you're going to give presents, you've got to get the presents you're going to give. At least, that's what women tell me. They tell me it's called "shopping."

However all the presents get under the trees and in the stockings, by the time we get them out of the stockings and away from the trees and unwrapped, most of us are exhausted. We are exhausted from the preparation for Christmas—and the anticipation of it. Even children, who don't do a lot of preparing for Christmas, are pretty exhausted by now from all their anticipation of it—even though they thought it would never get here.

But it did. Christmas has come, and this is the Sunday after. And now, a bit worn out by all the preparation and anticipation—and celebration—we have time to review and evaluate. We have time to consider the impact—and tally up the results.

The kids are already at it. Get two together and one of them will invariably ask the other, "What did you get?" When they go back to school next week, they will put the presidential pollsters to shame as they gather the collective data about who got what for Christmas.

But the kids aren't the only ones with the time to review and evaluate. Christmas has come—and we who have a few more Christmases under our belts will do our own inventories, in more subtle ways. We will tally up our Christmas, and our categories will be more sophisticated than those of our children and grandchildren.

You may have reached the stage in life where toys take a back seat to less tangible and more personal things, like the quality of your time with those you love. You may not be able to match the excitement of a four-year-old bounding out of bed on Christmas morning, but your heart can be filled with a joy that the little ones simply cannot imagine.

But let's take it deeper.

Christmas has come—which means Christ has come. And this is a good Sunday to consider the impact of His coming, and tally up the results, not of what we have given each other, but of what God has given us.

What presents did God give you, when all the preparations He had made across time were completed, and the centuries of human anticipation was fulfilled? What did you get for Christmas—from God?

Paul said, *"When the fullness of time had come, God sent his Son, born of woman, born under law."* He's talking about Christmas.

Here's what God gave you for Christmas. God sent His Son. You can send presents anywhere in the country. Give UPS or FED-EX a street address and they'll delivery your present right to someone's front door. On the other hand, God sent His Son to the womb of a woman—and to your heart and life—and He didn't need your zip code to do it.

We like to say: the greatest gift you can give is the gift of yourself. Here's your proof, infinitely magnified. The One Who was from-all-eternity-God, became as human as you can get, in order to give Himself to and for you.

But this was not one of those "What do I do with *this*?" kind of gifts. God's Christmas gift to you of His Son is a present with a purpose: *"God sent his Son…to redeem those who were under law."*

We better unwrap that a little bit because the world doesn't talk that way anymore. That's not to say it isn't true, it just means that we've denied and ignored the fact that we're "under law" so well for so long that most people are convinced now that we really aren't under it anymore.

And yet, there *is* a law that the world and all of us in it are under. This law is simply "the way reality works." It is the way God Himself set things up for the world He created, so that it and we would work together effectively on this planet.

We cannot eliminate, change or avoid this law of things. It determines the consequences of our actions as individuals and societies. To violate this divine law is to damage the processes God designed for productive and satisfying life on earth. It is, at the same time, to anger the Creator of this world Who has made us aware of this law's existence.

Every human being is subject to this law, and every human being (save One) has violated it. Every human being has suffered the consequences of our transgression against this law. We cannot keep this law and we cannot make it up to God for breaking it.

And so God sends His Son Who can both keep the law, and make it up to God, for us. In Jesus, for Christmas, God has given us redemption—at no small expense to Himself. He has paid, not just our bail, but the whole fine—in full.

What did you get for Christmas? The gift of God's Son—and the gift of redemption from your penalty under the law.

Now get this picture: You're locked up for something you did—guilty as sin and they got you dead to rights. Some nice guy comes along and gets you out and somehow also gets all the charges dropped.

Then instead of sending you on your way with a stern warning to do better next time and a little pocket change to get you by for a while, he takes you to his house to meet his dad, who, it turns out, was the one who sent the nice guy to spring you in the first place.

So you're pinching yourself and wondering how you got so lucky all of a sudden, and the guy's dad says, "Welcome home, son."

But he's not talking to the guy who paid for your freedom; he's talking to you: "Welcome home, daughter." "You don't have to go back to where you came from," the father is saying. "You don't have to live the life you've been living. My purpose in sending my son to free you was to adopt you as my own child. I'm giving you a new identity and a new future for Christmas. You will be my child—a member of my family—and you will share equally in all I have to give my children."[19]

❧❦

What did you get for Christmas?

The gift of God's Son, Jesus. Redemption from bondage to and punishment under the law. Adoption as a child of God.

---

[19] John 1:12-13.

Already it sounds like a MOLAB Christmas. That's MOLAB, spelled M-O-L-A-B, as in "made-out-like-a-bandit."

But there's more.

Paul says, *"Because you are God's children, God has sent the Spirit of his Son into your hearts."* (I mentioned that pinpoint shipping ability of God before.)

You got the gift of God's Son to redeem you from the terrible fix you were in. Then, after adopting you as His own child, God sends you the gift of the Holy Spirit like one of these "confirmation card" you get to assure you that you really are going to get the present promised to you. But God doesn't send the Spirit to your post office box or your front porch; the Spirit goes special delivery, straight into your heart.[20]

And the Holy Spirit isn't just sitting there watching the bowl games! He is creating fast, reliable and permanent connectivity between you and the Heavenly Father Who has adopted you as His very own. You don't have to walk around wondering, "Can He hear me now?" You have the Holy Spirit in your heart going, "Abba, Father!" all the time. And your "Abba"—your Father in heaven—is listening all the time—to you and the Holy Spirit in you—because you are His child—His beloved child.

৵৽৾

What did you get for Christmas?

You got Jesus, God's Son, sent to you.

You got redemption from the burden and penalty of the moral and spiritual law of the Creation that *none* of us can keep.

You got adopted as a child of God with all the benefits, privileges and promises due to a child of God.

You got the gift of the Spirit of Christ in your heart to confirm all the rest of it.

You made out like a—

---

[20] John 14:15-17; Romans 5:3-5.

O wait, there is a little "catch."

To get these Christmas presents, you have to accept them. You have to pull them out of the package they came in. Full stockings after Christmas are just silly. Unopened presents under the tree on Exhaustion Sunday don't make sense. Christmas has come.

Christmas has come. Christ has come—and He has brought you some wonderful gifts.

What did you get for Christmas?

What did you get from Christ?

❧

Galatians 5:1, 13-25 NRSV

¹ *For freedom Christ has set us free. Stand firm, therefore, and do not submit again to a yoke of slavery.*

¹³ *For you were called to freedom, brothers and sisters; only do not use your freedom as an opportunity for self-indulgence, but through love become slaves to one another.* ¹⁴ *For the whole law is summed up in a single commandment, "You shall love your neighbor as yourself."* ¹⁵ *If, however, you bite and devour one another, take care that you are not consumed by one another.*

¹⁶ *Live by the Spirit, I say, and do not gratify the desires of the flesh.* ¹⁷ *For what the flesh desires is opposed to the Spirit, and what the Spirit desires is opposed to the flesh; for these are opposed to each other, to prevent you from doing what you want.* ¹⁸ *But if you are led by the Spirit, you are not subject to the law.* ¹⁹ *Now the works of the flesh are obvious: fornication, impurity, licentiousness,* ²⁰ *idolatry, sorcery, enmities, strife, jealousy, anger, quarrels, dissensions, factions,* ²¹ *envy, drunkenness, carousing, and things like these. I am warning you, as I warned you before: those who do such things will not inherit the kingdom of God.*

²² *By contrast, the fruit of the Spirit is love, joy, peace, patience, kindness, generosity, faithfulness,* ²³ *gentleness, and self-control. There is no law against such things.* ²⁴ *And those who belong to Christ Jesus have crucified the flesh with its passions and desires.* ²⁵ *If we live by the Spirit, let us also be guided by the Spirit.*

৯০৩

3.

The Fruit of Freedom

Galatians 5:1, 13-25 NRSV

You're going to have a hard time with this sermon, I suspect. You're Americans, most of you, and this sermon is about freedom, and so you're going to think about freedom like Americans.

And that won't be helpful, because this sermon isn't about American freedom. It isn't about individual liberty and political independence. It isn't about patriotic parades and picnics in red, white and blue.

Next Sunday is the Fourth of July.

Today, we're gonna talk about a different kind of freedom.

You would have an easier time with the sermon if you could stop being Americans for a few minutes. In fact, you would help me a lot if you just pretended to be Galatians—new, Galatian Christians in the early years after the Crucifixion and Resurrection of Jesus. Will you pretend for a few minutes?

The amazing news of this amazing Man is spreading from Jerusalem and Galilee across the Roman Empire as fast and as far as soldiers and merchants and missionaries like the Apostle Paul can take it.

Paul has taken the news to villages scattered across Galatia, the central region of Asia Minor, and you and some of your friends have believed what he's told you about this Jesus, improbable as it sounds. You sat down with "Pastor Paul" and filled out the personal information sheet and posed for the pictorial directory—or whatever procedures he had you go through as you became members of this new church in Galatia.

But Paul's got to move on with the gospel, and so he sets up a few committees and hands out the pledge cards and off he goes. And there you are, wondering what you do now about this Lord Jesus the Messiah you just started believing in.

You could check your Bible, but the New Testament hasn't been written yet, and anyway, before long a bunch of guys from the "How to be a Real Christian Club" come along and tell you, "If you want to be a real Christian—a good Christian—you need to join the Jews."[21] It's what you might call "cutting edge" Christianity—which is a little tough, because most of you are not Jews.

You're just run-of-the mill Roman pagans—who now believe what Paul told you about Jesus. According to these new guys, you and your Galatian friends and neighbors need to start keeping the law in the Bible that does exist: the Genesis to Malachi part.

Well, somebody has the good sense to send to Paul and ask him about this before you give these guys the go-ahead to start the "initiation." And the letter Paul writes back comes sealed in an asbestos envelope, because when Paul hears what they're telling you—and that you're thinking about going along with it—he is hot! He is livid, in fact. Sparks fly from his pen and the ink is smoking on the parchment.

"Don't you dare!" he says. "Don't you believe them! Believing Jesus is the *only* thing you have to do to become a Christian."

And before he calms down, Paul writes you, *"For freedom, Christ has set you free! …do not submit yourselves again to a yoke of slavery."*

There's that freedom I was telling you about.

---

[21] Galatians 1:6-9.

But remember, it's not Fourth of July freedom; it's faith-in-Jesus freedom. You Galatians didn't win your freedom in battle like those Americans will in the 1770s and 80s. Christ has set you free by winning the battle against sin for you on the Cross,[22] in a real "year of our Lord."

Those Americans will fight courageously and persistently in their Revolutionary War for a freedom that will ensure them "life, liberty and the pursuit of happiness."[23] But Christ has given you freedom—has set you free—as a gift. It's already done. You had no part in making it happen.[24] You can only reap the benefits.

And the purpose for Christ giving you freedom is something even more important than any number of unalienable rights. Christ set you Galatians and all the other Christians free so that you will be free to do what God desires—free to walk in the Spirit and live in the Spirit—free to show love to other people as a way of showing love to God[25]—free to bear a special kind of fruit.

A lot of Americans will declare their freedom in 1776—and the rest will be declared free in the 1860s.[26] You Galatians are more like that latter group: You were freed from slavery—not a slavery to other men, though some of you have been slaves and some still are, in the earthly scheme of things.

But Christ set you free from a more important—more permanent—more pernicious—kind of slavery: slavery to sin.[27] Christ broke the bonds of sin that shackled you to condemnation in death and an eternity of torment.[28] Christ broke the bonds of sin and freed you from the life you were living as its slave.

---

[22] Colossians 2:15.

[23] Three unalienable human rights enumerated in the American *Declaration of Independence*, July 4, 1776.

[24] Ephesians 2:8-9.

[25] 1 John 4:11.

[26] *The Emancipation Proclamation* freed some slaves on January 1, 1863. The 13th Amendment, freeing all the rest in America, was ratified on December 6, 1865.

[27] Romans 6:17-18.

[28] Romans 8:1-2.

But interestingly enough, that's not what Paul is writing you about, all hot under the collar. Christ has set you free by His death on the Cross from the unnecessary obligation of well-meaning, but overbearing, religion. Christ died for you. Christ set you free. You don't have to do anything else to be saved. Just sign for "the package" and accept the gift: Just believe. *"Believe on the Lord Jesus Christ and thou shalt be saved,"*[29] as the old translation puts in.

Being bound up in sin is a slavery—and so is accepting an obligation to obey a system of unnecessary religious rules and regulations—letting other people shackle you with their expectations and additional requirements for being a real or genuine Christian.

You Galatians need to make sure you don't let anybody lay on more demands that Jesus did; otherwise, you'll slip right back into that slavery Jesus freed you from. You don't have to become Jews. You don't have to sign up for anybody's special spiritual system. Just do what Paul told you: Believe in the Christ Who set you free, and then use that freedom to live your life in the Spirit, bearing the fruit of the Spirit.

Christ has freed you from sin's unavoidable oppression on the one hand—and unnecessary religious obsessions on the other. That's what you've been freed from.

❧❦

But Christ has also freed you *for* something—and you know what? That "something" is not "whatever you feel like doing."

Doing whatever you want to do—whatever you can get away with—isn't really freedom. Take those Americans and what they will do with their freedom over the course of a couple of centuries: Their ever-expanding obsession with personal freedom, unconstrained by personal virtue or civic responsibility, will finally turn their dearly-purchased "life, liberty and pursuit of happiness"

---

[29] Acts 16:31, KJV.

into a culture of death, addiction and the perversion of happiness, all to prove that they will accept no restrictions on what they can do with their freedom.

But you—Paul says you have been "freed for freedom"—by Christ Himself—"called to freedom," by God Himself.

You're free, but you've got to do the right thing with your freedom or you'll end up slapping the shackles back on yourself, falling from freedom back into slavery. You're free, but you're not free to throw it all away.

You're free to love your neighbor. You're free to approach every experience in your life with joy. You're free to be at peace inside with the assurance of the Holy Spirit in every circumstance. You're free to be patient when nothing is going your way, and everybody is *in* your way. You're free to be kind instead of mean, good instead of evil, faithful instead of deceptive or unreliable. You are free to control yourself rather than cutting loose to see what you can get away with or how much you can get of the things you selfishly want.

You are free to follow Jesus, every moment of every day—free to walk in His Spirit and do all the things He wants you to do—all the things He made it possible for you to do. Freedom is God's gift, but it is not an "end-result" gift—it is a "means-to-an-end" gift—a preliminary, enabling gift—a gift given in order to make it possible to attain another, even better and more valuable gift—the opportunity to live a life pleasing to God and in harmony with His purpose for you.

❧

You see, it's not really *your* freedom—it's *God's*.

God has given you this Christ-won freedom for *His* purpose—to enable you to walk in the Spirit and avoid the slavery of the desires of the flesh—to bear the fruit of the Spirit—the only acceptable fruit of spiritual freedom.

So dig in your heels and don't let anybody tell you you've got to do more—or something else—to be a Christian. Stand firm when "the plan of the day"[30] calls for abusing the freedom God gave you and Christ restored to you, just so you can see how much personal gratification you can shove into the trophy case of the flesh.

❦

Well, enough pretending. You're not Galatians and it's not 55 A.D. Yes, you're Americans, most of you, and you're getting ready to celebrate the heroes of this country and the battles they fought for your freedom.

But there remains a different kind of freedom—a more important kind of freedom—won by the ultimate Hero of our faith. That Hero—that Christ on the Cross—set us free, and in this case, we proclaim our spiritual freedom by a declaration of *dependence* on Him.

"No thanks!" to the Law with all its oppressive demands.

"No thanks!" to the way of the flesh and the sinful, enslaving works that go with it.

"Thank God!" for the freedom He has given us, and for the fruit of the Spirit that will grow when we exercise that freedom—that freedom to which we have been called.

❦

---

[30] "The Plan of the Day" in the Navy is the general schedule for each day's activities in a command. It is written down and read out to all hands as they stand in formation before the workday begins.

Galatians 5:1, 13-25 ESV

¹ For freedom Christ has set us free; stand firm therefore, and do not submit again to a yoke of slavery.

¹³ For you were called to freedom, brothers. Only do not use your freedom as an opportunity for the flesh, but through love serve one another. ¹⁴ For the whole law is fulfilled in one word: "You shall love your neighbor as yourself." ¹⁵ But if you bite and devour one another, watch out that you are not consumed by one another.

¹⁶ But I say, walk by the Spirit, and you will not gratify the desires of the flesh. ¹⁷ For the desires of the flesh are against the Spirit, and the desires of the Spirit are against the flesh, for these are opposed to each other, to keep you from doing the things you want to do. ¹⁸ But if you are led by the Spirit, you are not under the law. ¹⁹ Now the works of the flesh are evident: sexual immorality, impurity, sensuality, ²⁰ idolatry, sorcery, enmity, strife, jealousy, fits of anger, rivalries, dissensions, divisions, ²¹ envy, drunkenness, orgies, and things like these. I warn you, as I warned you before, that those who do such things will not inherit the kingdom of God. ²² But the fruit of the Spirit is love, joy, peace, patience, kindness, goodness, faithfulness, ²³ gentleness, self-control; against such things there is no law. ²⁴ And those who belong to Christ Jesus have crucified the flesh with its passions and desires.

²⁵ If we live by the Spirit, let us also keep in step with the Spirit.

ও•৻

Matthew 7:15-20 ESV

[Jesus said:]

[15] *"Beware of false prophets, who come to you in sheep's clothing but inwardly are ravenous wolves. [16] You will recognize them by their fruits. Are grapes gathered from thornbushes, or figs from thistles? [17] So, every healthy tree bears good fruit, but the diseased tree bears bad fruit. [18] A healthy tree cannot bear bad fruit, nor can a diseased tree bear good fruit. [19] Every tree that does not bear good fruit is cut down and thrown into the fire. [20] Thus you will recognize them by their fruits."*

෧෪

4.

Free to Bear Good Fruit

Galatians 5:1, 13-25; Matthew 7:15-20 ESV

Go into a grocery store, and the first place you come to is probably the Product Section. The first thing you're likely to see is fruit—apples and oranges, bananas and grapes—lemons, limes, peaches and pears. If they do their job right, the produce managers will almost overwhelm you with their wonderful array of fruit—fresh fruit—good fruit—desirable fruit.

Good fruit is desirable—because it is good. And knowing that, the folks who put the produce out are quick to take the bad fruit away, or at least hide it out of sight at the bottom of the pile. People are looking for good fruit.

Of course, good fruit doesn't show up in the grocery store by accident. People from all over work hard to harvest good fruit, package it and transport it to the store. Before that, they tend the trees upon which the fruit will grow. Fruit trees produce fruit after their kind, and good trees produce good fruit. That's how it is—and how it's always been.[31]

And for that reason, both Jesus and the Apostle Paul use the image of fruit and the trees that produce fruit to talk about the

---

[31] Genesis 1:11-12.

Christian life. Jesus points out that the fruit growing from a tree will tell you what kind of tree it is: Apples grow from apple trees—oranges from orange trees. Simple, but significant.

And Jesus also points out that the quality of the fruit that grows on a tree will reveal the condition of the tree: The fruit a healthy tree produces will have to be good fruit and cannot be bad fruit. Again, obviously true, and yet deceptively profound.

In the end, Jesus is focused on the importance of the health of the tree and the kind of tree that is capable of producing good fruit.

ಶಿ✦ಳಿ

The Apostle Paul comes at the matter from a different direction. Paul points to the wonderful fruit produced by a particular kind of tree and contrasts this remarkable fruit with anything produced any other way.

And if the fruit tree is the image of mankind, its ability to produce good fruit is not something it can accomplish on its own.

Paul is not saying to people—to Christians: "Produce good fruit." He is not saying to you: "Be loving, joyful, at peace." He is not saying, "Be patient, kind, good, faithful, gentle, and self-controlled; or be these things more than you have been."

What he is saying is that you cannot *be* these things in and of yourself, no matter how hard you try.

Under normal conditions, you don't have it in you to produce that kind of fruit—good fruit. Under normal conditions, the fruit you can produce is so awful—so rotten—it isn't worth calling it "fruit."

Paul calls it "works"—*"works of the flesh"*—what results when you and everybody else in the world do exactly what you—we—feel like doing. His offhand list is long and ugly—and a pretty fair summary of the world we live in today and watch on TV every night—underwritten by corporate sponsors eager to advertise on the coattails of the moral corruption played out in shameless detail before our increasingly jaded eyes. It makes sense that, in an anything-goes world, "everything-that-comes" will not be the best of what's possible, but the worst.

But here's the surprise: The rules, regulations and restrictions of religious legalism don't produce good fruit, either. There is no more love, joy, peace, or any of the other stuff Paul listed as fruits of the Spirit, in servitude to all the laws in the Old Testament than there is in wild and total rebellion against them. Neither Law[32] nor license produces good fruit...

...which is why Paul is a fanatic about the freedom from the Law Christ's death made possible. *"For you were called to freedom, brothers..."* he tells the Galatians. If he were emailing them, I suspect this part would be in "all-caps" and bold face type with an abundance of exclamation points.

"Called"—by Whom? *"...to freedom"*—from what—and for what?

☜☞

The Crucifixion of Jesus—and His ministry that preceded it—was God's call, to any who would believe in Jesus, to shed the shackles of their stifling, suffocating servitude to a system of rules that rendered a loving, living relationship between God and anyone beyond anyone's reach. Like He did with Lazarus, bound up and laid away in a grave to rot, Jesus comes and calls to everyone bound up in legalism, "Come out!"[33]

And just as Jesus commanded the people around Lazarus to remove what bound him and let him go free, so Paul had heard the Risen Christ command him to bring that same freedom to everyone Jesus called.[34] And despite the opposition he ran into

---

[32] I have capitalized "Law" when referring to the Jewish legal system as a whole. When referring to individual requirements of the Jewish scriptures, I have used the lower case (law[s]).
[33] John 11:38-44.
[34] Acts 9:1-16.

everywhere, Paul proclaimed that freedom. He proclaimed freedom from the Law.[35]

Keeping the Law—to be of any value—had to be done perfectly—which it could not be.[36]

And if the Law could not be kept perfectly, keeping it imperfectly accomplished nothing in terms of overcoming the breach between you and God. That breach would be—and was— overcome only by God's act of grace in Jesus as it never could be by any act of sinful man.[37]

Paul proclaimed freedom from the Law—but not freedom for lawlessness. Both the Law as an end in itself, and lawlessness— moral license—as a law unto itself, are forms of slavery rather than freedom.

But as soon as he used the word, Paul followed it up with an equally stern warning: *"...do not use your freedom as an opportunity for the flesh...."*

How easy it is to hear "Freedom!" and think, "Anything goes!" But you know better.

❧

The freedom Jesus gives to all who answer His call is not a freedom "to do whatever you *want*." It is the freedom, finally, "to be able to do what you *should*." It is the freedom to let God do what you cannot do—to let God grow His holy fruit in you.

When Paul lays out a list of virtues to contrast the vices he stacked up on the "rap sheet" of the world, he isn't telling you to behave better. Of course, he's certainly not telling you to cut loose and behave badly, either.

What he is saying is that the characteristics of godly virtue can blossom in your life—not because you have the ability to bring

---

[35] Romans 8:2.
[36] James 2:10.
[37] Ephesians 2:8.

them forth—but because God's Spirit can grow this kind of "fruit" in you. And will.

And that is because before the fruit of the Spirit becomes the glorious evidence of the Holy Spirit's presence and activity in you, it is, and has always been, the fruit—*of* the *Spirit*.

Love, joy, peace, patience, kindness, goodness, faithfulness, gentleness, and self-control are aspects of God Himself, as Father, Son and Holy Spirit. They are aspects—though not the only ones—that operate eternally within the very nature of our God. And the evidence of these fruits of the Sprit reveals things about this God to us that suggest what He is doing in His interaction with us—and the traits that He desires to develop in us as part of the redeemed and sanctified nature into which He desires to transform us.

ঔ⊷ও

We've been talking about the fruit of the Spirit, but Paul mentions the Spirit a half-dozen times in these few verses in Galatians—and each time, in a slightly different way. He talks about the fruit of the Spirit—and the desires of the Spirit. He says, *"the desires of the Spirit are against the flesh"*—the physical, self-centered, sinful and all-too-human urges that rule so much of our lives and our world. That makes sense.

But have you ever considered that the Holy Spirit—God—has desires—things that God wants—and presumably exerts Himself to obtain?

Certainly, the desires of the Spirit are against the desires of the flesh—so that when you are tempted by the ways of the flesh, you're not the only one wanting you to overcome that temptation. The Holy Spirit desires that victory for you as well. Bearing the fruit of the Spirit requires walking by the Spirit, which means being led by the Spirit, which results in your keeping in step with the Spirit as you live by the Spirit.

You don't produce the fruit of the Spirit; the Spirit produces it in you. Choosing to move through life—to confront the challenges of each day—in harmony and companionship with the Holy Spirit is to walk by the Spirit—to desire what the Spirit desires. The Spirit does not desire to follow you—especially if where you choose to go is after the desires of the flesh that seduce you into thought and deed unworthy of the Spirit.

The Holy Spirit desires to lead you so that wherever you go you will find yourself in the kind of moral and spiritual climate where you can bear the fruit of the Spirit. And when you walk with the Spirit so faithfully that He is always leading you, you eventually find yourself, not just walking with the Spirit, but walking *in step* with the Spirit, stepping where He has stepped, even as a soldier might walk safely through a minefield by putting his feet where his leader put his and so marked the way.[38]

The way of the flesh is a minefield, full of danger for the wayward soul. One false step—one poor choice—one wrong move—and all the promise and possibility of life are blown away in an instant.

But the promise and great possibilities of life are safe and secure when you walk by the Spirit and live by the Spirit.

After you are freed from the Law, there are two ways in life—the way of the flesh and the way of the Spirit. Life in the Spirit bears good fruit. What life in the flesh bears is all too clear and not worth mentioning.

You are free to choose the way you will go. Christ set you free from the Law and lawlessness. Follow the Spirit and, *with* the Spirit, bear much fruit.

&⸱&

---

[38] This image was suggested by the story of General Norman Schwarzkopf's efforts as a battalion commander in Vietnam, intentionally entering a minefield in an attempt to rescue several soldiers trapped there.

From the Letter to the Ephesians

Ephesians 1:3-14 NRSV

³ *Blessed be the God and Father of our Lord Jesus Christ, who has blessed us in Christ with every spiritual blessing in the heavenly places,* ⁴ *just as he chose us in Christ before the foundation of the world to be holy and blameless before him in love.* ⁵ *He destined us for adoption as his children through Jesus Christ, according to the good pleasure of his will,* ⁶ *to the praise of his glorious grace that he freely bestowed on us in the Beloved.* ⁷ *In him we have redemption through his blood, the forgiveness of our trespasses, according to the riches of his grace* ⁸ *that he lavished on us. With all wisdom and insight* ⁹ *he has made known to us the mystery of his will, according to his good pleasure that he set forth in Christ,* ¹⁰ *as a plan for the fullness of time, to gather up all things in him, things in heaven and things on earth.* ¹¹ *In Christ we have also obtained an inheritance, having been destined according to the purpose of him who accomplishes all things according to his counsel and will,* ¹² *so that we, who were the first to set our hope on Christ, might live for the praise of his glory.* ¹³ *In him you also, when you had heard the word of truth, the gospel of your salvation, and had believed in him, were marked with the seal of the promised Holy Spirit;* ¹⁴ *this is the pledge of our inheritance toward redemption as God's own people, to the praise of his glory.*

ॐ∙ॐ

5.

Saying a Mouthful

Ephesians 1:3-14 NRSV

If Paul were writing Ephesians today, in English, he could not get away with this passage. It's 250 words in the English translation. It's 200 in the Greek—its original language. It looks okay now, but don't let the periods fool you. It's all one sentence. If Paul were writing the passage today, in English, the English teachers would flunk him.

In Paul's day, some 1950 years ago, a sentence like this was highly prized as a polished rhetorical device. It would have immediately impressed those who heard it—and everyone in the churches would have heard it because all reading was done out loud. It would have impressed the one who was reading it out loud, for, because it was one sentence, he would have been expected to read it all in one breathe.

By making it all one sentence, Paul was signaling that everything he said in it—all the thoughts expressed in the various subordinate clauses he wrote—was related.

But even reading it in English—with periods—it's still hard to understand. What holds it together if it's all "one thing"?

The clue is a little phrase that turns up (with occasional slight variations) throughout the passage. The basic phrase is "in Christ."

It turns up first in verse 3, where Paul tells us that God has blessed us with every spiritual blessing available to heaven—"in Christ."

In verse 4, we shift to the pronoun "Him," but the point is the same: God chose us "in Him" (meaning: "in Christ") before the foundation of the world to be holy and blameless in God's presence.

Verse 5: God destined us to be His children "through Jesus Christ"—another variation on the theme that means the same thing.

Verse 6: God freely bestowed His glorious grace "in the Beloved"—the Beloved, again, being Christ.[39]

Verse 7: "In Him," we have redemption through His blood, the forgiveness of our trespasses.

(Skip verse 8—the first verse in the passage where the phrase doesn't appear.)

Verse 9 is a little tricky: Either, God has made known to us "in Him" the mystery of His will that He set forth, or, God has made known to us the mystery of His will that He set forth "in Him." Either way, the important thing is that it is "in Christ" and it relates to everything else God is doing for us "in Christ."

In verse 10, Paul puts another piece of the puzzle in place: God's plan for eternity—*"the fullness of time"*—is to unite all things in heaven and on earth "in Him."

Verses 11 and 12: "In Him," "we"—the first generation of Christians—were destined and appointed to live for the praise of His glory.

Verses 13 and 14: "In Him," "you"—all succeeding generations of Christians—were marked with the seal of the promised Holy Spirit, the pledge of your inheritance as God's own people.

---

[39] Mark 1:11.

All this, "in Christ." All this—divine blessing, divine election, divine adoption, divine grace freely and generously bestowed, redemption, forgiveness, supernatural understanding, cosmic unity, eternal inheritance, continual presence of the Holy Spirit—all this is ours as Christians because we are "in Christ."

All that God has done and planned to do from all of eternity past—all that God is planning to do and will do throughout eternity future—has been done and will be done *through* Christ Jesus, and through Him, to us, because we are, as Christians, "in Christ."

How can you express all that in one lifetime, let alone in one sentence—in one breathe? And yet, there it is. You can sit in amazement at this run-on sentence, or you can live in amazement (and in praise) that you live—now and always—with all that it means—in Christ.

Ephesians 1:15-23 ESV

¹⁵ For this reason, because I have heard of your faith in the Lord Jesus and your love toward all the saints, ¹⁶ I do not cease to give thanks for you, remembering you in my prayers, ¹⁷ that the God of our Lord Jesus Christ, the Father of glory, may give you the Spirit of wisdom and of revelation in the knowledge of him, ¹⁸ having the eyes of your hearts enlightened, that you may know what is the hope to which he has called you, what are the riches of his glorious inheritance in the saints, ¹⁹ and what is the immeasurable greatness of his power toward us who believe, according to the working of his great might ²⁰ that he worked in Christ when he raised him from the dead and seated him at his right hand in the heavenly places, ²¹ far above all rule and authority and power and dominion, and above every name that is named, not only in this age but also in the one to come. ²² And he put all things under his feet and gave him as head over all things to the church, ²³ which is his body, the fullness of him who fills all in all.

෨ᚗᚑ෩

6.

Seeing with Your Heart

Ephesians 1:15-23 ESV

I yearn to preach the good news of Jesus Christ every Sunday. However, my eagerness was tempered somewhat this week as I came up against the challenge of this passage in Ephesians.

Here is the Apostle Paul at his best—or worst—depending on how you look at it. Paul is dealing with the deep things of the gospel, at which Paul is "the best." But Paul can go so deep into the depths of our faith that most people have a hard time following him. You know what I'm talking about: "Wow! That really sounds inspirational! I wonder what he said."

Let's see if we can figure out what Paul is saying. There's a clue in the first two verses.

Paul is describing his prayers for these Christians who are reading his letter. He gives thanks for their shared faith in the Lord Jesus and their love for each other.

From thanksgiving, Paul turns to intercession. He prays that God will give them a spirit of wisdom and revelation in the things of God, and that God will enlighten the eyes of their hearts. Paul goes on to list three very remarkable things that can only be seen with the eyes of the heart, and then his prayer ends with praise to God, for raising Jesus from the dead, and also for placing Jesus on the highest throne of heaven, with all the glorious things His eternal presence there means for us, the Church.

The passage deserves an extensive, detailed, in-depth explanation, but there will be an offering taken later and I've learned my lesson about lengthy sermons. So let me pull out one bright jewel from the treasure chest of Paul's thought process and hold it up to the light: Paul prays for light—divine light—for the eyes of their hearts.

ॐঃ৹

Yesterday, I went to a delightful 50th anniversary celebration. One of the couple's grown children wanted to read a tribute to her parents, and she stepped over to a window because she needed the best light available to illuminate her notes. You need physical light to see with your physical eyes.

But that is not the only way you see—or it shouldn't be. Even more important than what you see with your eyes is what you see with your heart. And seeing with your heart requires the kind of light that illuminates "heart vision." That kind of light does not come from a window, unless it is a window into your soul.

Paul prays that God will give his readers a spirit of wisdom and revelation. Revelation is what God shows you that you wouldn't and couldn't know any other way. Revelation is having a divine light turned on that illuminates something real that human eyes cannot see, and human wisdom does not know or understand or believe. Revelation is God's light for the eyes of the heart.

ॐঃ৹

You may have read that the conventional light bulb we have known all our lives is being phased out and will be unavailable within a few years. Science has come up with something new— something they think is better. Something similar is in the works for spiritual light.

42

For thousands of years, God has been providing a supernatural light for the eyes of the heart. And all that time, God's people have been seeing His revelation.

But over the years, more and more of those who are wise only in the ways of the world have been pushing a new kind of light, the light of human logic, the light of science and technology, the light of human progress. The goal is to extinguish the old light—the light of the heart—the divine light—and remove it from the marketplace of human experience. They think they have something better.

But nothing else works like the old light—the light of God's revelation. Nothing else will enlighten the eyes of the heart. And there are things God wants you to see, that you can only see with your heart.

❦

What are you seeing with your heart these days?

I'm seeing remarkable parallels between the experience of this fellowship and the children of Israel in the Bible. I'm seeing a people called out of an environment of oppression and spiritual blindness and worldly power and set on a course of radical dependence on God. I'm seeing the unexpected survival of a powerless people who were given a new identity as a community and launched on a pilgrimage with nothing to hold on to but their faith in the God Who is leading them somewhere else and providing for them just enough and just in time with each new step they take along the way.

My heart sees what Paul saw in the people to whom he wrote: a shared faith in the Lord Jesus and a godly love for one another in the fellowship. Shared faith and shared love: A good place to start.

But what now? What's next?

A lot of practical details. A lot of hard work and harder decisions. A lot of cooperation and patience and some forgiveness, too. A lot of wilderness wandering—or so it seems.

But the wilderness journey is also the path to a spirit of wisdom. God reveals Himself to His people in the wilderness in ways they never knew before. God gives a vision for the eyes of the heart to see that will show them the way to the place God has prepared for them.

What you see with your heart, enlightened by the revelation of God, will shed the necessary light on those practical details and decisions as well. Your heart will see how the practical fits into the supernatural plan of God for us. God will enlighten the eyes of your hearts with His revelation and divine wisdom, but you must open the eyes of your heart[40] to see what God would reveal to you. Otherwise, you are not looking in the light of the knowledge of God, but into the darkness of your own desires.

⁂

How do you know the difference?

Paul says that your heart, enlightened by God, will see several things.

When you open the eyes of your heart, you will know the hope to which God has called you. God will reveal to you where you're going. And the vision will be so wonderful that every sacrifice He requires will be worth it. The point of the journey is not leaving where you came from; it is getting to where you're going. The spiritual vision your heart sees sustains you through all the physical and emotional sacrifices the journey requires.

Your heart will see the incredible value of what God has waiting for you. I'm going to heaven and my mind cannot imagine what I will experience there. But my heart sees it. We're going somewhere as a new church, and my heart sees a vision of what

---

[40] Paul Baloche, "Open the Eyes of My Heart," 2000.

God has in store for us. Can I give you our future address or draw a picture of the permanent place of worship God will give us? No, but my heart sees that God has prepared a glorious inheritance for us—in this world as well as the next.

Hope. Inheritance. And incomparable power.

My heart sees that the God Whose power raised Jesus from the dead—and raised us from the dead—will put that power at our disposal for the accomplishment of His purpose for us.

Look with your eyes and you will see what we lack and what we have lost.

Look with you heart and God will reveal to you what He has given us and will give us. Look with your heart and you will see that you are not just folks holding forth in a makeshift facility; you are the body of the Risen and exalted Christ, the physical presence and spiritual representatives of the Ruler of all Creation and all eternity. Look with your heart and you will see Who Your Lord and Savior is.

Look with your heart and God will reveal to you who you are to Him.

The people Paul wrote were just starting out on their spiritual pilgrimage together. Paul had been in the wilderness[41] and knew what lay before them: hard times and a long journey.

But anybody could see that.

Paul saw more. Paul saw faith and love and the power of God poured out upon them. He saw the destination to which they were headed and the glory that would be theirs when they got there. Paul saw what God revealed—to the eyes of the heart. And he prayed they would see it, too.

Open the eyes of their hearts, Lord. Open the eyes of their hearts—and ours.

⊱⊰

---

[41] Galatians 1:15-17.

Ephesians 1:15-23 ESV

[15] For this reason, because I have heard of your faith in the Lord Jesus and your love toward all the saints, [16] I do not cease to give thanks for you, remembering you in my prayers, [17] that the God of our Lord Jesus Christ, the Father of glory, may give you the Spirit of wisdom and of revelation in the knowledge of him, [18] having the eyes of your hearts enlightened, that you may know what is the hope to which he has called you, what are the riches of his glorious inheritance in the saints, [19] and what is the immeasurable greatness of his power toward us who believe, according to the working of his great might [20] that he worked in Christ when he raised him from the dead and seated him at his right hand in the heavenly places, [21] far above all rule and authority and power and dominion, and above every name that is named, not only in this age but also in the one to come. [22] And he put all things under his feet and gave him as head over all things to the church, [23] which is his body, the fullness of him who fills all in all.

க⸱ை

7.

Far Above All

Ephesians 1:15-23 ESV

The day before yesterday, most of us, in some way or other, celebrated the independence of our country. We are "independent" in the sense that no other country controls our country. No other government governs it or determines its laws or dictates its affairs. And none ever has—since our ancestors threw off the yoke of authority exercised by a foreign power when our independence was won.

But we do not so much celebrate our *government's* independence as we do our personal independence as citizens of this country. There are many independent nations in our world today whose citizens have little or no independence at all. And even our country, powerful as it is, cannot force other countries to provide their citizens the freedoms even non-citizens enjoy in ours.

In this country, we enjoy the power to pick our own leaders. And yet, many of us are often unhappy with the way the leaders we pick exercise the power we place in their hands. Still, compared to the other options in operation in our world, having the population to be governed pick those who will govern them remains, we think, the best way for those who govern to obtain the power to do so.

When we celebrate on Independence Day, we seldom focus on our government. More often, we focus on our land and our people. We highlight qualities other than—and in addition to—independence. We praise our nation's natural beauty and abundant resources. And we celebrate noble character traits that we associate with our people, and positive values we think we share.

Certainly, we live in a land of limitless splendor, capable of supplying all our needs. But with the passage of time, we have seen the character of our culture change. Traits and values that were once on the dark margins of public life have moved to the mainstream, marking a departure from our traditions and the development of a society that will become less likely to sustain life and liberty, because of its growing obsession with the pursuit of personal happiness, selfishly defined.

❧

So, have I chosen to substitute political commentary for the proclamation of the gospel today?

No, but I have tried to paint one piece of a puzzle before presenting the bigger picture.

The world in which we live—the politics that play out before our eyes—the moral transformation running roughshod across our culture—all these things that trouble us—are but part—and only a small part—of a remarkable reality that is infinitely greater. And the point today is to put that problematic part of the picture into perspective within the wider scene.

❧

The Apostle Paul is doing a little celebrating of his own in the passage from Ephesians we just heard. He writes to faithful followers of Jesus Christ and celebrates their "Dependence Day."

And when, from his perspective, is Christian Dependence Day?

It is the day God raised Jesus from the dead—and more importantly—seated Jesus at the right hand of God in heaven.

Now, understand what that means: Paul is not saying that Jesus was lucky enough to get a "good" seat when He got back to heaven after going through all that unpleasantness on the Cross. To be seated *"at the right hand of God in heaven"* is to be given by God—not just a good seat—but the greatest "seat" in all the universe. And because God is a righteous God, giving Jesus this greatest seat means that it is the "right" seat for Jesus. It is only "right" that God would give the greatest seat to the greatest Guy—the greatest Guy ever.

It is the greatest seat in heaven, which is the realm of the eternal, which means that Jesus will occupy this greatest seat in all the universe—for all eternity. It will never *not* be His seat because there will never be anybody else greater than Him who will deserve it more.

⇛„≪

But this is not just about "sitting." The seat God has given Jesus is much, much more than the best seat on "the Observation Deck of heaven." The point is not just that Jesus have the best "view" in all Creation. The seat in which God has seated Jesus is the seat of ultimate authority. Jesus will not merely "see" everything from this seat; He will judge everything—control everything—rule over everything—in heaven, and on earth.

The Power that is able to raise a Man from the dead, and raise Him to heaven, and make that Man Ruler and Judge of all Creation, is a Power against which no other power can compete.

It possesses an authority to which all other authority must submit. Jesus now and forever sits in the "seat" from which ultimate, infinite, divine power is exercised.

Paul says all the power and authority of God has been given to Jesus, which places Jesus *"far above all rule and authority and power and dominion."* That includes every power or authority that is now, or ever has been, or ever will be, present on this earth—every empire, nation, state or city—every tribe, clan, family or individual—every corporation, company, club or clique.

It includes every power or authority beyond this world—or beyond the control or claim of anybody in this world. That includes powers like pride, greed, envy and lust—like fear, shame, pain and death.

The Power that raised Jesus from the dead has placed Jesus far above all these powers and any others that anybody could think up—or as Paul put it, *"above every name that is named, not only in this age but also in the one to come."* Even in your imagination, there is nothing and nobody who isn't far below Jesus and His power and authority.

❧

Paul lived in an age when power—whether political, military, economic or sexual—was generally exercised like a blunt instrument, without subtlety or finesse. Warriors beaten in battle were forced to prostrate themselves before the victorious general who placed his foot upon their necks to demonstrate to all their complete subjection. Civilian officials governed from elevated thrones so that those under their authority would also, physically, be "under their feet." And so to hammer home to Christians the truth about the unassailable superiority of their Risen Lord, Paul paints a picture of a Jesus under Whose feet God has placed all things.

We like to think of our country as the most powerful country in the world. Maybe we are. Maybe we're not. We know that we don't rule the world. We don't have anything like that kind of authority. We couldn't "take on" the whole world and ever hope to win. We don't have that much power.

But Jesus our Savior and Lord does. God has given Him that kind of power and authority—and infinitely more. God has given

Jesus all authority over everything in all Creation. And with that authority comes the power to make that authority stick.

Every country that concerns us—every politician that perturbs us—every trend that troubles us—every policy that arouses our negative passions—all of these are subject to the authority of Jesus. They will all lie prostrate under His feet. No one can claim "diplomatic immunity" with Jesus. No power is beyond His jurisdiction. All things—*"all rule and authority and power and dominion"*—are under His feet. God put them there when He pulled Jesus out of the grave and placed Jesus right there at His right hand in heaven.

☙⚬❧

And God did something else.

God gave Jesus to the Church to be Head of the Church—just like He is Head of everything else. In other words, the Church— the people who put their faith *in* Jesus and are faithful *to* Jesus— are as important to God as all the rest of His Creation combined. God made Jesus Head over all things—*and*—Head over the Church. These are His two "commands"—His two cosmic responsibilities.

Did you hear what I said—I mean, what Paul said?

God has given Jesus—the Risen Jesus—the eternally and infinitely exalted and all-powerful Jesus—to the Church—to head it up—to lead it and give it life—to protect it and empower it, which He is completely capable of doing. And that's what Jesus is doing, right here and right now—today in this place.

He is our Head—and we are His Body. Now, that part may be a little harder to actually get your mind around. But you know that the body does what the head of the body tells it to do.

My head is telling my body right now, "Finish the sermon." Your head may be telling your body, "Stay awake until he does."

Jesus, the Head of the Church, is telling His Body, the Church, all the things it needs to know and do—by His power and under His authority—to be His healthy and productive Body.

And Paul says that the Church—as the Body of Jesus—is filled with Him—because He fills everything. Jesus fills you and He fills me and He fills every Christian and every church and the whole Church with His power and authority, so that instead of a deadly independence *from* Him, we can enjoy a lively and lovely dependence *upon* Him, saved *by* Him and subject *to* Him in every wonderful way—joyfully subject to Him Who is *"far above all."*

ॐ•ॐ

Ephesians 2:12-22 ESV

[12] *...remember that you were at that time separated from Christ, alienated from the commonwealth of Israel and strangers to the covenants of promise, having no hope and without God in the world.* [13] *But now in Christ Jesus you who once were far off have been brought near by the blood of Christ.* [14] *For he himself is our peace, who has made us both one and has broken down in his flesh the dividing wall of hostility* [15] *by abolishing the law of commandments expressed in ordinances, that he might create in himself one new man in place of the two, so making peace,* [16] *and might reconcile us both to God in one body through the cross, thereby killing the hostility.* [17] *And he came and preached peace to you who were far off and peace to those who were near.* [18] *For through him we both have access in one Spirit to the Father.* [19] *So then you are no longer strangers and aliens, but you are fellow citizens with the saints and members of the household of God,* [20] *built on the foundation of the apostles and prophets, Christ Jesus himself being the cornerstone,* [21] *in whom the whole structure, being joined together, grows into a holy temple in the Lord.* [22] *In him you also are being built together into a dwelling place for God by the Spirit.*

৵৽৽৶

8.

No Longer Strangers

Ephesians 2:12-22 ESV

NO FOREIGNER IS TO ENTER WITHIN THE FORECOURT AND THE BARRIER AROUND THE SANCTUARY! WHOEVER IS CAUGHT WILL HAVE HIMSELF TO BLAME FOR HIS SUBSEQUENT DEATH.

৵৽৽

This is the wording of an inscription on a stone tablet found by archeologists digging around Jerusalem in 1871.[42] The Jewish historian Josephus, writing a little after the death of Paul, said this warning was posted on a wall in the temple compound, in Greek and Latin, well back from where the sacrifices took place.[43]

The "foreigners" the sign referred to were not people who lived in faraway lands, for Jews from all over the world were welcome to come to Jerusalem and into the temple courts to offer

---

[42] The tablet, known as the "Temple Balustrade" or the "Soreg" inscription, was discovered by French archeologist Charles Simon Clermont-Ganneau, and is now housed in the Istanbul Archaeology Museums in Turkey. See Jodi Magness, *The Archaeology of the Holy Land: From the Destruction of Solomon's Temple to the Muslim Conquest.* Cambridge University Press, 2012, p. 155.

[43] Josephus, *Antiquities of the Jews*, Book 15, Chapter 11, Page 5.

their sacrifices to God.[44] The sign made the wall a barrier to "spiritual" foreigners, people who were not Jewish, even if they lived in Jerusalem itself.[45] The Jews called these folks "Gentiles," and considered them farther away from God than even the dividing wall in the temple suggested.

Paul and the other apostles—and even Jesus Himself—had seen this warning sign when they went up to Jerusalem to worship in the temple. Being Jewish, they had all walked right past it to join the covenant community that gathered before the holy altar of God.

And then one day, Jesus saw that the Gentiles couldn't even get as far as the dividing wall on the temple grounds. The money changers and sacrifice sellers had turned the area behind the sign into an open-air market. He "dealt" with that problem—immediately.[46]

Years later, Paul and some Jewish friends almost got the penalty the inscription promised when they wandered beyond the wall, and a bunch of Jews around them decided Paul's friends weren't Jewish after all. Paul and his pals got out alive, but just barely—and just because the Roman guards nearby got there quickly enough to break up the bedlam that broke out.[47]

Paul may have had that "near-death experience" in mind when, while awaiting his execution in Rome, he wrote to some Gentiles Christians in Ephesus, reminding them of another, even greater dividing wall of hostility that their Savior Jesus had broken down for them. Paul told his Ephesians friends—whom he had apparently not met in person—what a good deal they have gotten as Gentiles from the God of the Jews.

ॐ

---

[44] Isaiah 43:1-7.
[45] Ezekiel 44:9.
[46] John 2:13-16.
[47] Acts 21:17-36.

But to properly appreciate what that means for the present and the future, you have to start with the way things were in the past. Paul, a Jewish Christian, says, *"Remember...*there was a time when you were not Christians, you were merely Gentiles."

And so it was for most of us.

There was a time when we were not Christians—not inside—not in our heart and soul.

There was a time when we really were "far off" from God, separated by our sin from Christ.

How does Paul put it? Alienated from the long and elect heritage of the children of Israel and God's chosen people, who moved through history in their special relationship with Him. Alienated—because we didn't belong—we weren't Jewish.

Can you remember being a stranger to every divine promise you now hold dear—and to the God Who made those promises to you? And if you cannot remember that time—then imagine it. Imagine having no hope, whatever your circumstances. Imagine being without God—totally without God—in the world—in *this* world!

There was a time when that was you—if you aren't Jewish. That was you—then.

❧

"But now..."

Two simple words. One thing changes and everything changes. *"But now—in Christ Jesus."* Paul, the Jewish Christian is writing to Gentile Christians, about their new and incredible "now"—in Christ Jesus. Just like in the temple, Jews like Paul were near to God, while Gentiles were far away. And Paul has pointed out how very far away from God Gentiles truly are.

But there's something else: No matter how much nearer to God Jews like Paul were, none of them were, or are, near enough to do any good where it really matters. Without Jesus, it's: "close, but no cigar"—and no salvation. Both Jews and Gentiles needed to be singing, "Nearer, My God, to Thee."[48]

"But now—in Christ Jesus"—you who were terribly far away from God, and Jews who were merely not near enough to God, have both been brought near and near enough—*"by the blood of Christ."* Unless you are in Christ Jesus, you are not near enough to God to make it matter.

☞❦

You see, there was another, more significant dividing wall of hostility in the temple in Jerusalem Paul knew so well. It was not a wall that divided one kind of person from another. It was not a human barrier based on differences of heritage or race or religious ritual. It was a far higher (in fact, insurmountable) wall of righteousness separating sinful man from holy God.

Its symbol was the great veil, or curtain, that blocked the way of even the Jews from approaching the presence of their God.[49] On one side—the sinful masses. On the other side—the Sacred One. And between the two—always a wall characterized by mutually repelling hostility.

Until—Paul says—Christ broke down the barrier—destroying the division and eliminating the hostility—in His flesh—by His blood—through His Cross.[50] The Jewish Christian Paul writes and tells the Gentile Christians, "He (Christ) has made us both one. He has created one humanity in place of two. He has reconciled us both to God. He has provided both of us—Jew and Gentile alike—a never-before-possible access to God the Father."

---

[48] Sarah Flower Adams, "Nearer, My God, To Thee," 1841.
[49] According to Josephus, *Jewish Wars*, Book 5, Chapter 5, Page 4, §212-214, the outer curtain of the temple was an 80-foot-high Babylonian tapestry of vivid colors that "portrayed a panorama of the entire heavens." See David Ulansey, "The Heavenly Veil Torn: Mark's Cosmic Inclusio," *Journal of Biblical Literature*, Vol. 110, No. 1 (Spring 1991), pp. 123-125.
[50] Matthew 27:45-51.

So where has the hostility between Jew and Gentile come from over the past almost two thousand years?

Not from God. Not from the Father Who sent His Son to break down that barrier by bathing it in His blood. Not from God, even if those who claim to be His followers perpetuate it in His name.

That's why Paul paints Jesus as the Peace Maker—the Peace Proclaimer—as Peace Itself: *"…he himself is our peace."* In Him, we experience a *"peace that passes understanding."*[51] By Him, we are given a peace the world cannot give.[52] From Him, we receive a blessing on our peacemaking,[53] an act of godly righteousness that confirms our status as children of God who have been brought beyond the once insurmountable dividing wall of hostility between us and God.

Then—you were in a hopeless, faraway, godless place.

Now—you are *"in Christ Jesus,"* near to God with open access to Him, and reconciled to your neighbor and God—no longer in a state of hostility with either. You were strangers—foreigners—outsiders regarding everything that mattered.

You are no longer strangers—no longer aliens. You are citizens as fully as anybody else in the kingdom of God. You are as much a child of God as anyone else He claims as family.

So what is Paul—the fanatical Jew who was determined to protect Judaism by persecuting Christian Jews (until he encountered the Risen Christ)[54]—Paul, the Apostle to the Gentiles[55] who retained his love for his Jewish heritage[56] (while

---

[51] Philippians 4:7, KJV.
[52] John 14:27.
[53] Matthew 5:9.
[54] Acts 8:1-3; 9:1-6.
[55] Acts 9:15-17.
[56] Romans 9:1-5.

refusing to impose the Jewish Law on Gentile Christians[57])—what is Paul telling these Gentile Christians in Ephesus about their identity and heritage in Christ?

"You are built on the foundation of the (Jewish) apostles (of the New Testament) and the (Jewish) prophets (of the Old Testament), with Jesus Christ Himself (also and necessarily Jewish) as the Cornerstone—the Anchor—and Jesus is holding the whole structure of what God is doing—of which you are now a full and functional part—together.

"And what you are a part of is not static or stationary. You are growing into a holy temple in Jesus. You, who couldn't have gotten within decent praying distance of God without Christ Jesus, are now being built into a place where God Himself will dwell—a place built by God's Holy Spirit Himself."

৫৯৬

Today, some nineteen and a half centuries after these words to these Ephesians were written, you may think of yourself (as a Gentile Christian) more like the Jews thought of themselves, in the Jerusalem temple and throughout the Roman Empire. You and I can become so accustomed to being religious "insiders" that we look askance at those around us, Jew and Gentile alike, who live their lives far away from God.

But remember that Jesus did not shed His blood to create another division in the ranks of sinful humanity. He died on the Cross to create a new humanity: like Him, without division, either from God or neighbor. There is nothing that any "outsider"—any non-Christian—needs from God that we, who by God's grace are now *"in Christ Jesus,"* did not need from God ourselves in order to go from being helpless strangers and hopeless aliens to enjoying full spiritual citizenship and the special status of God's beloved children.

---

[57] Galatians 2:15-16.

But neither are we to become complacent about those who, in our day, are content to remain *"strangers and aliens"*—who do not realize how far they actually are from God—and how disastrous that distance truly is—both now and for all time and eternity to come.

Paul could have been satisfied—as many of his Jewish Christian contemporaries were—to restrict his missionary efforts to *"the lost sheep of the house of Israel,"*[58] where Jesus began the work of bringing all mankind into the glorious presence of God. But Paul was not satisfied, and so you and I were told that the good news of Jesus Christ was for us, too.

And because of Jesus Christ, we are no longer strangers.

And because of Christ, no one else need be, either.

৵৽

---

[58] Matthew 10:5-6; 15:24.

Ephesians 4:1-16 NRSV

[1] *I therefore, the prisoner in the Lord, beg you to lead a life worthy of the calling to which you have been called,* [2] *with all humility and gentleness, with patience, bearing with one another in love,* [3] *making every effort to maintain the unity of the Spirit in the bond of peace.* [4] *There is one body and one Spirit, just as you were called to the one hope of your calling,* [5] *one Lord, one faith, one baptism,* [6] *one God and Father of all, who is above all and through all and in all.*

[7] *But each of us was given grace according to the measure of Christ's gift.* [8] *Therefore it is said,*

> *"When he ascended on high*
> *he made captivity itself a captive;*
> *he gave gifts to his people."*

[9] *(When it says, "He ascended," what does it mean but that he had also descended into the lower parts of the earth?* [10] *He who descended is the same one who ascended far above all the heavens, so that he might fill all things.)* [11] *The gifts he gave were that some would be apostles, some prophets, some evangelists, some pastors and teachers,* [12] *to equip the saints for the work of ministry, for building up the body of Christ,* [13] *until all of us come to the unity of the faith and of the knowledge of the Son of God, to maturity, to the measure of the full stature of Christ.* [14] *We must no longer be children, tossed to and fro and blown about by every wind of doctrine, by people's trickery, by their craftiness in deceitful scheming.* [15] *But speaking the truth in love, we must grow up in every way into him who is the head, into Christ,* [16] *from whom the whole body, joined and knit together by every ligament with which it is equipped, as each part is working properly, promotes the body's growth in building itself up in love.*

☙❧

9.

One

Ephesians 4:1-16 NRSV

When you open a Bible, you see a lot of words. It's what you expect to see. But you also see something else—though you may not realize it. You see a lot of numbers, and I don't mean just chapter and verse and page numbers. There is an entire book of the Bible called Numbers, and it lives up to its name. There are a lot of numbers in the Bible.

Some of these numbers turn up over and over, suggesting they have some special importance. Three is a fairly common number in the Bible.[59] So is seven.[60] Ten is big for commandments and cured lepers.[61] Twelve is a perennial favorite for Old Testament tribes and New Testament disciples.[62] There are forties[63] and fifties[64] and hundreds[65] and even thousands[66] scattered about. But

---

[59] Daniel 3:23; Jonah 1:17; Matthew 26:34; Mark 9:5; John 2:19.
[60] Genesis 2:2-3; 2 Kings 5:7-9; Matthew 18:21-22; Revelation 1:4.
[61] Exodus 34:27-28; Luke 17:11-14.
[62] Genesis 49:28; Matthew 10:2-4.
[63] Genesis 7:12; Joshua 5:6; Matthew 4:2; Acts 1:3.
[64] 2 Samuel 15:1; Luke 9:14.
[65] Genesis 21:5; Proverbs 17:10; Matthew 13:8.
[66] Exodus 18:25; Psalm 50:10; Matthew 14:21; Mark 5:13.

the most important number, if Ephesians is any indication, may be the number one.

As you heard, *"there is one body and one Spirit."* There is *"one hope, one Lord, one faith, one baptism, one God and Father of all."* That's a lot of very important *ones*. *One* turns up in other places, of course. Jesus says in the Gospel of John that *"I and the Father are* **one.** *"*[67] Later in John, Jesus prays that His disciples will be *one* in the same way.[68] *One* is a very important number.

In Ephesians, as in other places in the Bible, *one* is important, but it isn't always really "one" in the strictest sense. In Genesis, Adam and Eve are *two* who become "one" in marriage.[69] In Matthew and other places in the New Testament, the Father, Son and Holy Spirit are *one* God in *three* Persons.[70]

Here in Ephesians, the one Body is the Body of Christ, the fellowship of all believers with Christ, an ever-growing number of people unified by their saving experience with Christ and their ongoing fellowship in Christ. The point of the emphasis on "one" is not the splendor of the individuality of one person, even in the glory of personal salvation. The more important point is the unity—the "one-ness"—that is possible in Christ for so many.

❧

Christians are not saved to be set adrift in splendid spiritual isolation from all other Christians, to enjoy some private pilgrimage with God. We—you and I—have been redeemed from our sinful separation—from God and our neighbors—so that we may be unified—put back into the reconstituted and corporate family of God. Christ died to make each of us right with Him— and being right with Him, to unite us with Him—so that He could then unite us all with each other in Him.

---

[67] John 10:30.
[68] John 17:11.
[69] Genesis 2:24.
[70] Matthew 28:19; Romans 8:9; 2 Corinthians 13:14.

If you think of yourself when you think of "one," you have the wrong number. If you are not making every effort to maintain the unity of the Body, to make yourself a part of this Body, you are setting yourself up as something other than the Body, and therefore ensuring that there will always be more than "one." There will be you, and there will be the Body that God intends for you to be a part of, but aren't.

That's why we emphasize membership here so much. It's not that we need the total number of members to be higher. It's that God wants the membership to be "one."

God wants us all united—in the Holy Spirit—as one Body—with Christ (our one Lord) as the Head. Becoming a member of a church is a way of identifying yourself with the Body. It is a way of saying to yourself and to the other members and to God that you are seeking that unity He has called you to seek and to share.

ॐ

The alternative is to stand apart and aloof in your heart and soul—to *not* be "one" with the Body as God desires and intends and Paul begs you to be. Are you a part of the Body—or are you merely attached to it or associated with it? Are you part of the unity of the Body—or are you separate and apart from it?

You cannot live a life worthy of your Christian calling if you are living it as a solitary Christian, separate from the Body of Christ. Being separate is dangerous spiritually. It is as dangerous for a Christian in the spiritual realm as it is for many animals in the physical realm.

If you ever watch documentaries about wild animals, they will usually show you how the predator stalks its prey. Those most vulnerable to the predator's attacks are those individuals hanging around the fringes of the flock or herd, or those who have wandered off entirely. It turns out that there *is* safety in numbers and the safest place is well inside the whole. It's true on the savannahs of Africa and the steppes of Asia. And it's true within the unity of the Body of Christ.

Unity is the goal of the church's ministry and the measure of a church's maturity. God wants one people with one Head, and He always has. The Holy Spirit is making unity possible, bringing about and maintaining the unity of the church.

ॐ

But if unity is God's goal for us as a congregation, the goal of the enemy of God is our dis-unity. God's enemy would like nothing better than to foster conflict and factions among us. This enemy will do everything within his power to achieve this ungodly goal.

Just as the Holy Spirit invites, encourages and enables each of us to be a genuine part of Christ's one Body, the devil constantly challenges each of us to see others and ourselves as not a part of the whole—as separate, disconnected—not "one" with God or His church, in this place or any other.

Just as God is at work in powerful and exciting ways to build up this church, you can be sure that we will not escape the clever and alluring efforts of Satan to neutralize as much of the Holy Spirit's work among us as possible. Stand by—it's coming! One minute you will be inspired by some aspect of our ministry here, and the next, you may find your feelings hurt by someone or your thoughts disturbed by some practice or plan.

The devil is lurking—waiting for some opening to nurture an attitude—to stimulate an action that will bring down the building-up work of the Spirit. How little it takes to pull us away from the unity of faith in the bond of peace!

It's not a new thing. God united the man and the woman in the garden and made them one flesh[71]—and the devil tempted them into a sinful isolation from each other and from God.[72] God

---

[71] Genesis 2:21-24.
[72] Genesis 3:1-24.

provided their children the special unity of brotherhood, but despite God's warning to Cain: *"Sin is crouching at the door; it's desire is for you, you must master it,"*[73] Cain chose in his anger and jealousy to separate himself from his brother in the most complete and permanent way possible.[74]

ୠ୦

So analyze every impulse: Will this impulse in question unify and strengthen the Body, or will it weaken the fabric of faith, and fragment the fellowship?

Consider every action: Will this act build up the Body (and me as a part of it) or will it tear us all down? Is this an act of love on my part? Love is, after all, the atmosphere that allows unity to live and breathe.

We are responsible to grow in unity. The effort to do so is our common vocation as believers. We are called to the life of Christ and to life in Christ. And we are not left alone to achieve this goal through our own efforts.

All the gifts of Christ are given for the building up of the Body. These spiritual gifts are individual in nature, but they are corporate in purpose. They are intended by God for unifying the Body in the power of the Spirit. This building up of the Body is what you might call the ultimate or strategic purpose for the giving of spiritual gifts.

The building up of the Body of Christ is to be accomplished by equipping the saints for the work of the ministry. This is the immediate or tactical purpose for our various spiritual gifts.

Your commitment to the Body as a member of this church is an example of your determination to make the number "one" the most important number in your relationship with God.

The humility, gentleness, patience and forbearance you show your fellow Christians, and your church as a whole, demonstrate your recognition that "one" is the most important number.

---

[73] Genesis 4:7.
[74] Genesis 4:8.

Another way you demonstrate your commitment to unity is in communion. The word itself conveys that sense of "oneness" we are called to embrace. The first syllable, "com," means "with." "Communion" becomes "comm-union"—"with union"—or unity. When we break the bread and pour the wine—when we gather side-by-side—shoulder to shoulder—to receive by the grace of God and the power of the Holy Spirit what our Savior commanded us to receive, we create the holy sign that we are "one."

We claim different denominations, but we are "one." We worship at different times in different forms, and yet we are "one." We are different in so many ways, but we are all "one" in Christ— if we lead a life worthy of the calling to which we have been called, maintaining the unity—the "oneness"—in this Body of Christ.

∾∾

Ephesians 5:1-14 ESV

¹ Therefore be imitators of God, as beloved children. ² And walk in love, as Christ loved us and gave himself up for us, a fragrant offering and sacrifice to God.

³ But sexual immorality and all impurity or covetousness must not even be named among you, as is proper among saints. ⁴ Let there be no filthiness nor foolish talk nor crude joking, which are out of place, but instead let there be thanksgiving. ⁵ For you may be sure of this, that everyone who is sexually immoral or impure, or who is covetous (that is, an idolater), has no inheritance in the kingdom of Christ and God. ⁶ Let no one deceive you with empty words, for because of these things the wrath of God comes upon the sons of disobedience. ⁷ Therefore do not become partners with them; ⁸ for at one time you were darkness, but now you are light in the Lord. Walk as children of light ⁹ (for the fruit of light is found in all that is good and right and true), ¹⁰ and try to discern what is pleasing to the Lord. ¹¹ Take no part in the unfruitful works of darkness, but instead expose them. ¹² For it is shameful even to speak of the things that they do in secret. ¹³ But when anything is exposed by the light, it becomes visible, ¹⁴ for anything that becomes visible is light. Therefore it says,

> *"Awake, O sleeper,*
> *and arise from the dead,*
> *and Christ will shine on you."*

৯৵৹

10.

Not Even a Hint

Ephesians 5:1-14 ESV

In 1936, Adolph Hitler "re-militarized" the Rhineland, the region of Germany that bordered France, Belgium, and Holland. It was a flagrant violation of several treaties. In the spring of that year, Hitler sent a small force of several hundred men into the area to test the resolve of his neighbors.

His action was forbidden, but those threatened by it told themselves they were not threatened. They did nothing to oppose him, even though they could have stopped him easily —at the time. And because they did not confront the soldiers and "send them packing," more of Hitler's soldiers marched into the Rhineland to join the first contingent—and more followed them—until the nations of Western Europe faced an army on their border too large and entrenched to be challenged—until it was too hard to do anything—or so they thought.

And then, the day came when an overwhelming evil poured out of this place the appeasers of evil had tried to ignore. An evil erupted that turned their relatively peaceful world into the deadliest slaughter house ever seen. And when, in the end, this evil was defeated, another had been let loose to take its place that turned half a continent into a political prison where, for half a century, every citizen within lived and died under a crushing ideology of darkness.

In 1936, they had said to themselves: "It's just a minor incursion. It's easier just to let it go. What harm can it do?"

And what harm could it do to let a little bit of evil get a little foothold in a place where a lot of evil could do a lot of damage later on?

୧୭

Paul has the answer to that question—the question our world asks over and over today, not expecting an answer, but assuming that the question is its own answer—an answer very different from the one Paul presents to the Ephesians as he leads them, first, through the theological foundations of the gospel, and then to the gospel's practical, moral applications.

"Follow God's example," Paul says. "Walk in the way of love," he says. It all sounds so very warm and fuzzy—so spiritually inspirational.

And then Paul tells you what it means to follow God's example and walk in the way of love: *"there must not be even a hint..."* among you. There must not be even a hint—of *what*?

Well—of sexual immorality, any kind of impurity, or greed, to start with.

So let's start with these—these three evils that are not to be tolerated under any circumstances by those of us who are joined in a fellowship committed to following God's example.

In an earlier part of this letter, Paul promoted three traits among Christians: humility, meekness and patience. Now, Paul points to three behaviors and attitudes—to start with—that we are *not* to engage in, endorse, or even entertain the idea of.

Paul wrote his letters almost 2,000 years ago and our world is still beset with an epidemic of sexual immorality, impurity, and greed. Paul told his readers: *"It is shameful even to mention what the disobedient do in secret."*

What would he think today, where, thanks to the internet, cable TV, and unregulated movies and music, the number and fervor of "the morally disobedient" has reached the point that now the shameful things, previously done in secret, are proudly portrayed and promoted in public, every hour of every day, everywhere, for men, women and children to see—and celebrate.

જ~ક્ર

But the point of this sermon is not to gratify our sense of moral superiority. It is to recognize the guidance given to us in the Church who, though redeemed from our sinful, worldly works and ways, are still susceptible to their physical, emotional and psychological allure.

Paul says, *"...not even a hint...!"* He says this for two reasons.

One is to protect *us.* Jesus Christ died on the Cross to defeat our enemy: sin. He drove our enemy out of the territory the enemy had captured. He also drove our enemy out of the territory from which we could be invaded again.

We must not allow our enemy even to approach those places where we could be vulnerable to him. We must not let our enemy take up any position from which to assault us—or infiltrate us. We must confront and oppose the first effort and every effort of our enemy to reclaim any of the places in our lives Jesus fought so hard and gave His life to liberate.

"...not even a hint...!" Fight every temptation. Accept no compromise or negotiated peace with evil. Do not flinch from the resolute defense of your spiritually fortified moral positions—and ensure that they remain fully and properly fortified.

As the secular world—and too many in the Church who claim to be our allies while consorting with the enemy—systematically and increasingly undermine your traditional defenses, you must regroup and reestablish new defenses in cooperation with other Christians who share your commitment.

"…not even a hint—because these are improper for God's holy people." These things are not suitable for who you now are—they just don't fit you anymore—not even a little bit. They get in the way of your new relationship with God and your growing relationship with all the other people who are now your spiritual family here. They get in the way of what matters most. They put a distance you do not want between you and God.

"…not even a hint"—because they're *"out of place."* Sexual immorality, impurity, greed—and obscenity, foolish talk and coarse joking—and everything else that's just wrong for us because we are God's holy people—is also wrong because it's out of place.

And what "place" is it "out of"? The "place" that we are now "in" and "of": the kingdom of God. These behaviors and attitudes are not part of the culture of the kingdom of God. Think kingdom thoughts and do kingdom deeds and adopt kingdom attitudes and you will find yourself *"in place"* in the kingdom of God. Try to bring even a little bit of the world's ways into the kingdom and it just won't work—or work out.

But can we mount a "perfect" defense against sin—our old enemy whose weapons are the time-tested temptations to sexual immorality, impurity and greedy materialism?

No, even the most determined defensive line in this life will occasionally be breached. But every position must be manned at all times. And everyone who stands the watch must be constantly vigilant. And every invader that breaches the line must be repelled as soon as possible—even if it means calling in reinforcements—which it often will.

ॐ

…which brings us to the other reason Paul says, *"Among you there must not even be a hint"* of ungodly attitudes and actions. The best thing you can do for yourself as part of the Body of Christ is to live like you are the Body of Christ.

And the only way the world will finally wake up to the error of its ways is if somebody—or some Body—lives a noticeable and compelling alternative lifestyle to *their* alternative lifestyle, so that when it finally becomes impossible to ignore or evade the absolutely certain consequences of a life lived in collaboration with the enemy of all humanity, they will know where to run for refuge: where there isn't even a hint of those things the enemy used to destroy their lives.

The world, for its part, proclaims that it is neither healthy nor possible to resist sexual desire, even the immoral variety. In fact, the world has concluded that little of what the Bible, our common sense and proven experience have considered immoral in the realm of sexual activities and attitudes actually is immoral. And what little they still accept as immoral will likely be embraced as moral soon, in order to gain the accolades of the enemy's acolytes.

The same approach to impure thoughts and deeds and the desire to possess gets the same treatment from the world. "Greed is good," they say.[75] "Your opposition to 'impurity' is prudish and I have the right to think anything I like and do anything I like and 'push the envelope' as far as I can, regardless of the consequences for me or anybody else, since I refuse to acknowledge any consequences or accept any responsibility for them."

But these things are the marks of our world. Sexual immorality, physical, mental and social impurity, materialism, coarseness, gossip, and a host of other unholy habits that Paul alludes to elsewhere[76] are all around us every day.

❦

How do you avoid them? How can you get to *"not even a hint"* when the whole world is awash in them—when that's all you ever see and hear, try as you might not to?

---

[75] A line from Michael Douglas' character, Gordon Gekko, in the movie, *Wall Street*, 1987.
[76] Romans 13:13; Galatians 5:19-21; Colossians 3:5.

You make the hard choices. You do not compromise where it matters. And you make very sure you understand where God says, "It matters." If you must step away from the world to stay close to God, do so. If you must become different—do it—by becoming more like Christ—by the power and grace of His Holy Spirit, since you can't become different or more Christ-like by yourself.

છે‑જ્

There was a man who saw the march into the Rhineland for what it was, and he opposed it with every resource at his disposal. Though he could not stop Hitler in 1936, he would not allow even a hint of acceptance of the encroachment of evil. He shone a light into the darkness and exposed it for what it was.

And in Europe's darkest hour, this pudgy fellow with the bulldog scowl became a beacon of hope for all those who had let the evil go on too long. He told the world in his distinctive British accent, "We shall never surrender!"[77]

And they didn't.

છે‑જ્

Paul said something very interesting about why we are to take this business of our moral behavior so very seriously. He said, *"You were once darkness…"*

Not, "You were once *in* darkness." *"You **were** darkness."* You've heard of black holes in space. There are black holes in human souls as well.

"You were darkness, but now, you are light—in the Lord." You are not just *in* the light of our Lord—enjoying that wonder and glory of this new life and new hope and new power He has given you. You *are* light.

You have been saved from the darkness you were. You are now "illuminated" by the Light of the world, so that your life's

---

[77] Conclusion to a major speech Prime Minister Winston Churchill made in the British House of Commons on June 4, 1940.

light exposes darkness and its deeds—and lights the way for those who would come to the Light you reflect.

It's like Jesus said, *"You are the light of the world. A city set on a hill cannot be hidden. Nor do people light a lamp and put it under a basket, but on a stand, and it gives light to all in the house. In the same way, let your light so shine before men, that they may see your good works and glorify your Father who is in heaven"*[78]

Now, you are children of light. Do not accept even a shadow—even a hint—of the old darkness in your life. Live as children of light—as the light of Christ shines on you and radiates out from you.

❧

---

[78] Matthew 5:14-16, RSV.

Ephesians 5:21-33 RSV

[21] *Be subject to one another out of reverence for Christ.* [22] *Wives, be subject to your husbands, as to the Lord.* [23] *For the husband is the head of the wife as Christ is the head of the church, his body, and is himself its Savior.* [24] *As the church is subject to Christ, so let wives also be subject in everything to their husbands.* [25] *Husbands, love your wives, as Christ loved the church and gave himself up for her,* [26] *that he might sanctify her, having cleansed her by the washing of water with the word,* [27] *that he might present the church to himself in splendor, without spot or wrinkle or any such thing, that she might be holy and without blemish.* [28] *Even so husbands should love their wives as their own bodies. He who loves his wife loves himself.* [29] *For no man ever hates his own flesh, but nourishes and cherishes it, as Christ does the church,* [30] *because we are members of his body.* [31] *"For this reason a man shall leave his father and mother and be joined to his wife, and the two shall become one flesh."* [32] *This mystery is a profound one, and I am saying that it refers to Christ and the church;* [33] *however, let each one of you love his wife as himself, and let the wife see that she respects her husband.*

෴

11.

The "Submission Thing"

Ephesians 5:21-33 RSV

If you've watched the news on television lately, you've probably seen the reporters talk about this poll or that. If it is your habit to sit down to a quiet meal at the normal dinner hour, the pollsters have probably called you on the phone. These are "public opinion" polls.

I would like to conduct a "private" opinion poll with you this morning. I will ask you a question and I would like you to consider which of two answers you prefer. This is a "private" opinion poll because I do not want you to share your opinion with me. Decide what you think and keep it to yourself—to yourself and God.

The question is this: Is the Bible merely *inspirational*—a source of heart-warming devotional thoughts…to "brighten your day and lighten your way"? Or is the Bible also, and perhaps pre-eminently, *instructional*—an authoritative guide to thinking and acting in accordance with God's will?

If you are of the "Inspirational School," then you will be content to float from wonderful passage to wonderful passage, as the bee to spring blossoms, drawing sweet nectar where you find it, while ignoring those gardens where fragrant flowers do not grow.

But if your Bible is the Word of God with divine authority still, then you must till row by row in the biblical garden and harvest every plant so that no nutritious food is neglected.

The Bible's opinion on this question is stated pretty clearly: *"**All** scripture is inspired by God and profitable for teaching, for reproof, for correction, and for training in righteousness, that the man of God may be complete, equipped for every good work."*[79]

The Bible itself claims God's inspiration for every word in every verse in every book. Not every verse inspires, but every one instructs, and equips the submissive reader for all that God desires of him or her. Every passage is inspired by God and possesses God's authority.

ॐ

And with that fact comes a problem.

If you're just looking for inspiration, you can simply ignore all the troublesome passages—the passages you don't like. But what do you do with the passages you don't like if God doesn't want them ignored? The passage we read earlier is just such an example. It surely fits the bill for a troublesome, disliked, prefer-to-ignore scripture for many people

Almost nobody today, inside the church or out, wants to take this passage seriously. But there it is; still in the Bible. Is it still "authoritative"? Or have we "outgrown" it? Are we too modern—too sophisticated—to take it seriously anymore?

If the Bible is the inspired word of God, why would God have left this passage in there? It's a source of ridicule from the secular world. It's just about the most attractive target of radical feminists and other enemies of Christianity desperate to ravage the Bible's moral and spiritual authority. The modern, secular, feminist-driven culture rails against the idea of wives submitting to their husbands in marriage: "Insane! Barbaric! Patriarchal! Fascist!"

---

[79] 2 Timothy 3:16-17, KJV.

Now this is an interesting reaction when you consider their alternative. The secular folks promote a value system that encourages women to submit to any number of men outside of marriage. If a man wants to have sex with you, with no forethought or concern for the physical, emotional, medical, financial, or social consequences to you, let him, they say. Let him, whoever he is, use your body for his momentary pleasure with no expectation of responsibility for the results. Women are encouraged to put themselves at the mercy of selfishness, egotism, uncontrolled anger—and then rage about the damage men do.

With the epidemic of out-of-wedlock pregnancies and single parenting—or the callous encouragement to abort—the date rape and venereal diseases—the depression, debt, and shattered self-esteem, it's clear to see why the world would be so hard on a Christian model for marriage: their worldly way works so much better than God's. And you don't have to worry about God's will.

❧

But speaking of God: Did God set marriage up the way Paul writes in Ephesians out of spite for women? Does the Christian God despise and devalue women as much as the world accuses the Christian Church of doing?

The Gospels say, "No"—resoundingly! Jesus liberated women from the outdated straightjacket they wore consistently—everywhere and in every age—until Jesus.[80] And every day and every place since, every action by, for, and against women has been judged by the standard Jesus established for their fair and honorable treatment.

"Well, maybe Jesus is okay and Paul's the one who has the problem with women."

Please note: At no time does Paul suggest that men are *better* than women—or brighter. Paul does not say that men make better

---

[80] Luke 7:36-50; 10:38-42; John 4:1-27; 8:3-11.

leaders than women (though he certainly assumes that men will do the leading). He does suggest elsewhere that men are physically stronger,[81] which is a reasonable and accurate generalization.

Paul refers to women as the spiritual equal of men[82] and treats them as such.[83] Paul says women are free and equal to men in Christ and before God.

And he tells them to submit to their husbands.

ॐॐ

Most people think this passage makes no earthly sense at all today. Of course, God has never been particularly concerned with or impressed by "earthly sense."

All right, then, "Why would God make marriage to be this way?"

Let's consider a theoretical possibility: Perhaps the passage merely *looks* outdated, intolerant, reactionary, and disgusting—but, in reality, remains the inspired word of God. As such, it would not only retain divine authority over us—it would also contain divine blessings for us—if we obey it. Is it possible that there is a deeper truth buried beneath what only *seems* to be foolishness? Paul says, *"…the foolishness of God is wiser than men… God chose what is foolish in the world to shame the wise… so that no human being might boast in the presence of God."*[84]

Could this be God's way for marriage so that there will be no doubt that when it works, the glory will be God's and not yours—so that a successful marriage will be a miracle whose source can only be God?

Notice that Paul subordinates the purpose of marriage to the purpose of the Church in the passage we read earlier.

---

[81] Turns out that it was Peter who made that claim in 1 Peter 3:7, where he directs men to show honor and understanding to their wives—and all women.
[82] Galatians 3:28.
[83] Acts 16:11-15; Romans 16:1; Philippians 4:3.
[84] 1 Corinthians 1:25, 27, 29 RSV.

Now, do not interpret that idea of "subordination" to mean that all free time and every spare nickel is to be poured into your local church. It does mean that every marriage exists to strengthen the Church and to model to an ignorant, indifferent world what the Church is and what God is doing with it in the world.

Does the way you interact with your marriage partner—do the things you two devote your marriage to—promote the Christian community's impact for Christ in the world? Husbands and wives, you are the Church in your homes. You bring the Church here when you come here—and take it back with you when you go.

Unfortunately, most Christians and most churches in America today have, in practice, rejected this biblical model for marriage just about as completely as the secular world has. People may *be* Christians, committed in their personal lives to a saving relationship with Jesus Christ, dedicated to bringing the power and influence of the Holy Spirit into their homes and the lives of their children, and still reject the biblical model for their marriage relationship.

Too many Christian folks do the logic this way: "That 'submission in marriage' thing is just so weird and outdated that it can't be taken seriously today. But surely, we can make the secular model work because *we* are Christians. People who can't make a "go" of marriage must fail because they're trying to work the secular model without being Christians."

Wrong!

To paraphrase the politicians: "It's the model, stupid!"

The generic secular model for marriage is broken. It's defective. It doesn't work. And the more you adopt the overall godless value system and perspective of modern culture—the more the moral and spiritual defects of our culture filter, unnoticed, into your personality and behavior—the quicker you will come to chaos and grief in your secular marriage, whatever the thickness of the Christian veneer you apply on the surface.

So let's get down to business and unpack this "submission thing," and see why it's still God's word and God's will.

જ⊸⊰

First of all, please notice that at no point does Paul instruct husbands to force or demand submission from their wives. This is strictly between God and the wife. Husbands are instructed to love their wives as Christ loves the Church—and there'll be more on that next Sunday. Bring the men who need to hear it.

Paul also tells all Christians in verse 21 to be subject to each other. And telling husbands once appears to be enough for them. But Paul decides to emphasize the point to the wives: *"Be subject to [your husband] out of reverence for Christ. Be subject to your husband…as to the Lord."*

Wives, would you subject yourselves to your husband if your husband *were* Christ—rather than that particular example of manhood you freely and enthusiastically chose? How would your attitude, your tone of voice, your expectations be different if you were "Mrs. Christ" instead of "Mrs. Whoever-You-Are"? Would you begrudge Christ your submission? Would you wait to see if His behavior or demeanor deserved your submission? Would you measure submission to Him out carefully to ensure that it did not exceed what His attitude and actions had earned? Is that how you submit to Christ now? The Bible says, *"Submit to your husband as you submit to Christ."*

If you will not be subject to your husband, you cannot be subject to Christ. To be subject to Christ, you must subject yourself to your husband—as you do (or should) to Christ—as the Church does (or will) to Christ. And if you will not be subject to your husband as the Bible instructs you to do, what excuse will you give God? What excuse do you think God will accept?

To subject yourself to another, you must humble yourself and restrain the ego that yearns to be first and greatest. It requires maturity, strong character, and faith in the wisdom of the Holy One Who requires it.

This can be hard, for women are almost always the more spiritually mature—the more spiritually active partner in the marriage. And yet, the Bible says they are to subject themselves to their plod-along husbands.

Why? Is it to teach wives humility? (Notice I said "humility," not "humiliation." There is a big difference.) Is it to stimulate spiritual growth and commitment in the man who maybe wouldn't bother in these areas if he didn't have to? Maybe God doesn't want women "carrying" their men spiritually?

It's probably not because the husband is superior to the wife in exercising authority, either. But husbands generally *need* to exercise authority more that their wives do. What husbands need most is respect, the kind of respect that comes with being in charge of something important.[85] And Paul concludes this passage by insisting that wives *show* their husbands respect (not because they *are* respectable—Paul says nothing about that—but so that they will *want* to be, to prove your respect justified.)

What wives need most, on the other hand, is not respect, but love—Christ-like love. If the wife submits, she gives the husband what *he* needs most. If the husband loves her, the wife gets what *she* needs most. (And next week, we will get into how the husband is to love his wife.)

Wives, what does your submission do to your husband?

It humbles him. *You* know he doesn't deserve it. So does he. But you do it anyway. And it humbles him—and then it encourages him—it builds his confidence and determination to fulfill his sacred responsibility as a husband.

If there's a constant struggle for control in the marriage, husbands will generally take one of two approaches to it.

---

[85] See Emerson Eggerichs, *Love and Respect: The Love She Most Desires; The Respect He Desperately Needs*, Integrity Publishers, 2004.

Some will contend, and others will concede. Both options are losers.

If you're constantly wrestling for the upper hand or the last word, the marriage wastes the energy available to do great and necessary things. But not all husbands will struggle with their wives to see who gets to lead in the marriage. If you will not submit, your husband may.

Sound good? Think again.

ॐ॰॰ॐ

If your husband concedes to you the role God has directed him to fulfill, your husband will withdraw from his rightful responsibilities, and from you, in passive anger and unexpressed shame, in confusion, depression and indifference. He will look for other, less appropriate, places where he may lead—and perhaps other, less appropriate, people who will let him hold the position of leadership in their lives that he longs to hold in yours. And if he concedes authority to you, then *you* are the leader—the head—in change. But of what? Of an empty shell of a marriage? Of a family where you get to play both husband and wife?

Your husband is not likely to do his part if you don't do yours. It's not likely that he will be motivated to love you like Christ loves the Church when you are bent on taking his God-given role away from him.

So, by refusing to submit to your husband you've disobeyed God, demoralized your husband and piled all the responsibilities of marriage on your own shoulders. It would seem that just about everyone would be dissatisfied with this arrangement. Sounds like it's time to make a change—even if you are *exactly* where the world says you ought to be.

Before your husband became (or becomes) your husband, God put a system of marriage in place. God did this not because all men are better qualified—or that your particular man is. But it *is* the husband's assignment, regardless of whether you support him in it or not. The Bible says: *"The husband is head of the wife as Christ is head of the Church."* And both positions, your husband's and Christ's, are divine assignments. It's not a hierarchy of value; it is a remarkably wise and effective distribution of function.

The point of both assignments is not prestige or hubristic power, but responsibility. It is the weight of the responsibility imposed by God, and the life dedicated to sacrificial service to fulfill that solemn and sacred responsibility, that justifies the honor to be paid to the husband by the wife's submission. The husband bears the final responsibility before God for the spiritual, social, moral and physical condition of the marriage.

Not the wife—the husband.

And not because he is better suited, but because he is officially, divinely assigned. Withhold your submission and oppose any effort on his part to do his job—make it all but impossible for him to be your head—and he is still accountable to God for the job you won't let him, or won't help him, do.

"The husband is the head of the wife as Christ is head of the church." *Is*—not *ought* to be, or *could* be. This is a plain statement of completed fact. Like it or not—accept it or not—behave accordingly or not, the Bible says, *"The husband is the head of the wife."* It doesn't say, "…until the feminist movement of the second half of the 20th Century figures out that this is a sexist arrangement and shows intelligent people a better system."

Here's divine revelation for you: *"The husband is head of the wife."* No "ifs." No "buts." There are a few "ands," which we'll get to in time, but they do not restrict or qualify Paul's categorical assertion. This is a "done deal." God has willed it in His infinite wisdom, and in His equally infinite power, He has already made it so.

❧

So how does this submission work in practical terms?

Say an issue arises. And no clear-cut consensus response emerges. The wife says, "I think we ought to do *this*." The husband says, "I think we ought to do *that*." The wife knows the husband is wrong, but she cannot convince him. So she submits to him, knowing that his decision is wrong.

The result is the disaster she predicted. The husband is responsible. The wife is vindicated—and loyal—and the next time an issue arises with no clear-cut consensus response, she says with greater confidence—and equal submission—"I think we ought to do *this*." He says, "I think we ought to do *that*."

But he also thinks: "The last time we did this, she was right, but she let me make a choice that blew up in my face, even though I was convinced I was right. She trusted me, and I let her down. So maybe I ought to pay more attention to her perspective because she'll submit to my decision again and I don't want to mess things up again by not listening to her."

On the other hand, if the husband is right (which could happen) and the wife is wrong (a possibility, at least theoretically), she's had her say with no harm done and he succeeds in his responsibility, building his confidence in his leadership ability—and in her support. And she gets to praise and appreciate him for doing such a great job on her behalf.

You might say that submission is an "inspired" strategy for success in marriage.

❧❦

Now, all of this has important implications for those of you who have not yet become wives. If you are to subject yourself to the man you marry in all things as you do to Christ, you should be very careful and selective in your choice of a husband. Among your criteria for an acceptable mate—perhaps the most importance criteria—should be that *the man already submits to Christ* as you will submit to him.

Submission to anyone is not an easy thing. But if you must bend your will to another human being—and the Bible says wives must in marriage—you will be infinitely happier if that person has already bent his will to Christ. Whatever qualities—physical, financial, psychological, or social—a man possesses to attract and intrigue you, all of his qualities pale in significance to this one: his submission to Christ. And all the good you anticipate in a marriage will turn to bitter ashes without it.

If a man is not submissive to Christ, do not allow yourself to become subject to his charms. And, for goodness sake, do not assume that his submission to Christ will come *after* you marry him—or *because* you marry him. If you marry him, you are to be submissive, whether he is or not, so be wise and do not "go there" if the man is not where he must be spiritually to satisfy God as a husband for you.

And do not be submitting the things a woman should only submit to her husband before he *is* your husband. Do not share a man's bed or his home or his bank account if you are not married to him. A man who will have sex with you or live with you or use your money, without having married you first, does not love you as Christ loves the Church.

"But I *know* he loves me."

No! If a man will seek or accept this level of intimacy with you without—or before—being married to you, he does not love you as Christ loves the Church.

And by accepting the "benefits" of marriage from you without the public and sacred commitment of marriage, he calls into question whether he will become like Christ in his love to you just because he goes through a ceremony with you later that brings no significant change in the actual behavior already established in your relationship.

No, Christ would not do it—and a Christ-like man wouldn't, either.

Perhaps your man will protest, "But I *am* a Christian and I *do* love her!"

The definition of Christian has been stretched a bit in our day, even to the point of covering anybody who has a background in

Christianity or some positive feeling toward Whomever he personally perceives Jesus to be.

But the *biblical* understanding of a Christian seems to be: "a follower of Christ who lives in obedience to Christ's example and His word, not knowingly or persistently doing what is clearly contrary to the Master's will.

And the word "love" serves to label a host of very different attitudes and emotions, some of which are anything but what Christ demonstrates in His relationship to His Church.

So I shall repeat: A man who will relate to a woman as though she were his wife when she is not, is *not* a Christ-like man, and does *not* love this woman as Christ loves the Church.

Single women, beware.

୧୦ଛ

How can this biblical model, presented by Paul, work in our day?

It can work—and does—because God *wants* it to. It serves His greater redemptive purpose for the Church and humanity and all Creation. God *makes* it work.

Biblical marriages demonstrate the nature of the relationship between Christ and His Church. Biblical marriages are the seedbed of a new generation of Christians, the foundation of truly godly homes. Biblical marriages equip the husband and wife to grow in their personal relationship with God—as well as their relationship with each other.

Don't worry about justifying your submission to your friends who can't even begin to take the idea seriously. They've been brainwashed with the false assurance of superior understanding.

Don't worry about defending it to the world. Just do it for Christ, and see if God's way doesn't change the world, starting with your marriage.

୧୦ଛ

12.

And Now: The Husbands

Ephesians 5:21-33 RSV

Ladies, I think you can sit back and relax this morning. If the biblical spotlight glared down on wives last week, it will focus just as firmly on husbands today. But try not to enjoy yourselves *too* much. "Amens" are authorized in response to particularly relevant points. However, please try to keep the elbow jabbing to a minimum.

Look with me again at the passage we read last Sunday. Listen again to God's requirements for both husbands and wives:

❧

[21] Be subject to one another out of reverence for Christ. [22] Wives, be subject to your husbands, as to the Lord. [23] For the husband is the head of the wife as Christ is the head of the church, his body, and is himself its Savior. [24] As the church is subject to Christ, so let wives also be subject in everything to their husbands. [25] Husbands, love your wives, as Christ loved the church and gave himself up for her, [26] that he might sanctify her, having cleansed her by the washing of water with the word, [27] that he might present the church to himself in splendor, without spot or wrinkle or any such thing, that she might be holy and without blemish. [28] Even so husbands should love their wives as their own bodies. He who loves his wife loves himself. [29] For no man ever hates his own

flesh, but nourishes and cherishes it, as Christ does the church, [30] *because we are members of his body.* [31] *"For this reason a man shall leave his father and mother and be joined to his wife, and the two shall become one flesh."* [32] *This mystery is a profound one, and I am saying that it refers to Christ and the church;* [33] *however, let each one of you love his wife as himself, and let the wife see that she respects her husband.*

જ્જ

All right, husbands, let's get down to business.

The Bible here makes one assignment—and gives two orders for completing that assignment properly. Your divine assignment is to serve as head of your wife as Christ serves as Head of the Church. To become a husband is to become the head in your marriage. We talked about that last week. Let's do a quick review for the husbands who weren't here—or weren't paying attention.

Your assignment as head of the wife represents merely a distribution of function, not a hierarchy of value. The point is not prestige or hubristic power, but responsibility. At no time does Paul suggest that men are better than women, or brighter, or more effective leaders. But God has nonetheless assigned husbands the final responsibility for the spiritual, social, moral and physical condition of their marriage.

You may have been assigned this position in marriage because husbands generally *need* to exercise authority more that their wives do. But you are not told to demand or force submission from your wife. That's none of your business; it's between your wife and her God.

It may also be that God wants to stimulate your spiritual growth and commitment, rather than letting your wife, who may be more spiritually mature, "carry" you spiritually? You are not authorized to abdicate your place as head of the wife because you find the demands made upon you heavy or difficult to satisfy. Whatever your shortcomings—*you* got the job!

Consider: The captain of a ship may not be the best navigator on board, but the navigation of the ship is still, ultimately, his responsibility. And if the ship founders on the rocks, it is the captain who will be held accountable. Too many "marriage captains" are jumping ship at the first sign of rough waters, or hiding in their cabins while their "XOs"[86] or first mates struggle to run the ship and lead the crew alone. Husbands, depend on your wives and honor their support, but take charge as God requires you to.

❧

There are two orders given to husbands in the Ephesians passage. The first is so subtle, you could easily miss it: *"Submit to one another out of reverence for Christ."*

This does not authorize you to shirk your responsibility to be the head of your wife. But it does require you to submit to the refining influence your relationship with your wife will have on your life, your personality, and your faith. It also suggests something of the spirit with which you are to approach carrying out your assignment as head in the marriage.

The other direction God gives husbands is this: *"Love your wives, just as Christ loved the church."* It sounds easy: "Love your wife."

"Well, of course, I love my wife. That's why she is my wife. I fell in love with her and just couldn't imagine my life without her. I love the way she walks. I love the way she talks. I love the way she makes me feel."

Well, yes, that's love of a sort, but it's not really what the Bible is talking about. To satisfy God, you have to love your wife *"as Christ loved the Church."*

So how did Christ love the Church?

---

[86] The "XO," or Executive Officer, is the next senior person under the Captain, or Commanding Officer, in a naval chain of command. The "XO" is usually in charge of the practical management of the ship's activities each day.

Christ loved the Church by "giving Himself up" for her. He died saving the Church. He suffered—and bled—and died. And husbands are to do the same, if circumstances require. In various parts of the world today, they do.

☙❦

But before Jesus walked the Via Dolorosa[87] to the Cross—or bared His back to the "whip with teeth"[88] in Pilate's dungeon—He had already sacrificed His personal will on the altar of total obedience to God.[89] Before Jesus went to the Cross to save the sinners He loved, He went down on His knees in a simple dining room to wash their feet and demonstrate what we now call "servant leadership."[90]

Jesus gave up His professional aspirations and his privacy.[91] He gave up any chance to live in peace,[92] or to enjoy an ordinary life as "one of the guys" in Nazareth.[93] Jesus gave up self-centeredness[94] and easily-offended pride[95] and the normal perks of a leader.[96] Before that, He gave up His divine place and power in heaven to become a man[97] and devote Himself, body and soul, to His Bride, the Church.[98]

---

[87] The Via Dolorosa is a street within the Old City of Jerusalem that Jesus is believed to have taken on His way from Pilate's palace to the place of His crucifixion. The words are Latin. "Via" means "way" or "road." "Dolorosa" has been translated variously as "of grief," "of sorrow," "of suffering" or "of pain."
[88] This instrument of torture was comprised of a number of leather strips, attached to a handle at one end, and knotted at the other, loose end with pieces of metal or bone to rip the victim's skin.
[89] Matthew 26:39.
[90] John 13:1-16.
[91] Matthew 13:2; Mark 3:9.
[92] Matthew 10:34.
[93] Matthew 13:53-57.
[94] John 5:19.
[95] Matthew 11:29.
[96] Matthew 20:25-28.
[97] Philippians 2:6-7.
[98] 2 Corinthians 11:2.

"Husbands, love your wives as Christ loved the Church and gave himself up for her." The husband cannot hold tight to his own hopes and dreams and desires and pleasures as the most important things. He must give up his commitment to all these things as the driving motivations in his life. He must give "himself" up and embrace his wife as the focus and goal of his life, or he will not be loving his wife as Christ loved the Church.

The will of God is clear: *"Husbands love your wives as Christ loved the Church."* Don't bother checking how *you* feel about it. Just do it. Christ-like love is love you "do." It is an ongoing act of self-discipline. It generates incredible power and transmits that power through this love. What Jesus felt for the Church we may infer by what He did. He loved the Church in what He did for her.

The Bible is remarkably indifferent to "feelings" as the basis for deciding whether something should or should not be done. That's what the Law of God was for, and later, the Word of God in the person of Jesus and the writings of His early followers. Husbands, do what the Bible tells you. Your feelings will catch up in time, if they need to.

☜⚜☞

How do your love your wife as Christ loved the church?

The Bible says, *"Husbands should love their wives as their own bodies."* Your wives are a part of you. They are like your own bodies—and are to be treated as such. What do you do when you sprain your ankle or get the flu? Do you cut off the part of your body causing you pain and throw it away? Do you badger it, or smack it around? Do you give it the "silent treatment"?

No, you "attend" to it. You touch it gently and carefully. You think about it all the time and pray that the pain will go away and that its cause will be healed. Though you may hate what has happened, you don't hate your body for the suffering it's going through. It's your body and you just want it to get well. And you'll do whatever it takes to make that happen. Love your wife as you do your own body.

"Love your wife as Christ loved the Church." It's a hard command, when you know how you are to love. But the "how" will become easier when you understand the "why."

҈

Why does Christ love the Church?

Someone once said, "Christ does not love the Church because it is lovable, but rather to make it so."[99] The love of Christ is not determined by what the Church deserves, but by what God is, by His nature and His character, by His purpose for establishing the relationship between His only begotten Son and His only redeemed remnant. Christ loves the Church in order to make her holy.

The husband's Christ-like love is to sanctify the wife—to make her holy—to bring about growth in godliness. We don't use the word "sanctify" very much. What does it mean? It means, primarily, to set something—or someone—apart for a sacred purpose. Christ loves the Church the way He does so that He might sanctify her. A husband doesn't have the divine grace that Jesus had to save people from sin. A husband is not Christ. But a husband can be *in Christ*, and have Christ in him.

Paul says in Colossians that Christ *"is the image of the invisible God... For God was pleased to have all his fullness dwell in him, and through him to reconcile to himself all things...by making peace through his blood, shed on the cross."*[100]

---

[99] The correct wording of the quotation is "He [Christ] loved the Church not because it was perfectly lovable, but in order to make it such." The quotation is from Brooke Foss Westcott, *St. Paul's Epistle to the Ephesians: The Greek Text with Notes and Addenda*, New York, NY: The MacMillan Company, 1906, p 84. On the following page, Bishop Westcott wrote in a similar vein: "He [Christ] loved the church not because it was holy, but in order to make it holy by union with Himself."

[100] Colossians 1:19-20, RSV.

Husbands, Jesus is the Image of God to you—and you are to be the image of Christ to your wife. God is pleased to reveal Himself to your wife through you, as part of the reconciliation God is working in her. What better vehicle does God have to introduce His intention to have an intimate relationship with humanity than the most intimate human relationship—marriage?

A husband can receive the grace of Christ, and use it under the guidance of the Holy Spirit to bless—and even sanctify—the life of his wife, by seeing her and treating her as the divine creation she is. A husband can love his wife as Christ loved the Church—but only if Christ is helping him?

≈∘≪

There is a wonderful truth expressed in 2 Corinthians 5: *"From now on…we regard no one from a human point of view."* [101] This is to be especially true for the regard a husband has for his wife. Do you see your wife as Christ sees her? Are you trying to? Do you see or seek to see what Christ sees? Jesus said, *"Seek, and you will find."* [102] If you look for her beauty, for instance, you will find it and make it more apparent to the world.

On the other hand, if you overlook it, or deny it, or belittle it— if you just take it for granted—you will tarnish it and cause it to fade, no matter how brightly it shone at the first. The same is true of your wife's potential for holiness. You will not see who your wife will become so much as your wife will become who you see her to be.

"Sanctify," "cleanse," "splendor," "spotless," "holy"—these are divine terms. As head of the wife, the husband prepares his wife for her relationship with Christ and her eternal place in His presence. When you look at your wife—when you think about her—what spiritual things do you hope and dream for her? Can you imagine your wife as the woman God created her to be? Can

---

[101] 2 Corinthians 5:16, RSV.
[102] Matthew 7:7, RSV.

you imagine the plan God has for her—in this life and for all eternity? Can you imagine her spiritual need? And when she enters eternity, what part of her "spiritual readiness" will be attributable to you and your lifetime of Christ-like love for her?

The point of being "in charge" is to meet the needs and enable the success of those you love—those you lead and serve. Husbands, do you set aside your power and privilege to provide for your partner—to give her the grace gifts she needs to lift her up to her proper place in Christ?

A husband's primary witness to Christ is his relationship to his wife. In this, he tells his wife: "This is what the love of Christ for you is like. This is what you may expect from Christ as a part of His Church."

A husband's treatment of his wife will be the first and strongest lesson his daughter will learn about how she should be treated by the boys and men she encounters in her life—what she may expect, and what she should accept. A husband's treatment of his wife will be the first and strongest lesson his son will receive about how to treat girls and women he interacts with as he grows to manhood and seeks the one who will become his wife.

❧◈☙

Now, "for the information of all hands,"[103] there are wives among us today. One may be yours. Which kind of husband do you think your wife would prefer—the kind who would love her as Christ loved the Church, or the kind who merely loves her like the "what's-in-it-for-me" world around us?

What kind of husband would she be most willing to be submissive to? I suspect that even those wives who are less than enthusiastic about submitting to their husbands are very enthusiastic about the idea of being loved as Christ loved the

---

[103] The standard introduction in the Navy to announcements made on the shipboard public-address system, known as "the 1MC."

Church. Feel free to conduct your own opinion survey on this after the service.

And, after all that, is there no personal benefit to the husband who loves his wife as Christ loves the church?

Well, you get to love a woman better than you ever could if you were limiting your love to what you could generate from your own feelings with your own personal perspective on life. You get to participate in the work of Christ in your home in a direct and significant way—validating your very existence.

You get to spend your life with a woman who experiences the greatest form of human love available, and probably responds accordingly. You get to look yourself in the mirror every morning and respect what you see because you know you have been chosen to be—and have agreed to be—God's primary instrument of grace to the woman you love the most in life. And you get the indescribable joy of knowing that God loves you in the same way that you are committed to loving your wife—and that God is proud of you for obeying His word. All in all, not bad—for a husband!

"This is a profound mystery," says Paul. But don't let that stop you.

Love your wife—as Christ loves the Church—as Christ loves you.

Ephesians 6:10-20, NRSV

[10] *Finally, be strong in the Lord and in the strength of his power.* [11] *Put on the whole armor of God, so that you may be able to stand against the wiles of the devil.* [12] *For our struggle is not against enemies of blood and flesh, but against the rulers, against the authorities, against the cosmic powers of this present darkness, against the spiritual forces of evil in the heavenly places.*

[13] *Therefore take up the whole armor of God, so that you may be able to withstand on that evil day, and having done everything, to stand firm.* [14] *Stand therefore, and fasten the belt of truth around your waist, and put on the breastplate of righteousness.* [15] *As shoes for your feet put on whatever will make you ready to proclaim the gospel of peace.* [16] *With all of these, take the shield of faith, with which you will be able to quench all the flaming arrows of the evil one.* [17] *Take the helmet of salvation, and the sword of the Spirit, which is the word of God.*

[18] *Pray in the Spirit at all times in every prayer and supplication. To that end keep alert and always persevere in supplication for all the saints.* [19] *Pray also for me, so that when I speak, a message may be given to me to make known with boldness the mystery of the gospel,* [20] *for which I am an ambassador in chains. Pray that I may declare it boldly, as I must speak.*

ॐॐ

13.

Wrestling with the Devil

Ephesians 6:10-20 NRSV

Do you believe there is a devil? Many people—perhaps most—today do not. But Jesus did—and so did Paul. The Bible is full of the devil.

Disbelief is understandable: if there is a devil, he certainly doesn't want you to think so. C. S. Lewis wrote a very popular book in which the devil's disciples worked very hard to convince people the devil and his disciples didn't exist.[104]

But if there is a devil, you are at war—an undeclared, but very real war. It's not like physical wars between nations and human armies—though they often get dragged in. The devil's war against God and His children is universal in scope, unending in time, and spiritual in nature. It will not end until God ends it.

And since we are at war with the devil, Paul says, "Suit up!" Clothe yourself with the full armor of God—everything He has to give you: truth, righteousness, peace, faith, salvation, sacred scripture, Holy Spirit. Leave no bare spots, no undefended vulnerabilities. Put on everything God provides to protect you from everything the devil can throw at you.

---

[104] C. S. Lewis, *The Screwtape Letters*, 1942.

But realize, says Paul, that the devil will eventually "close" with you in hand-to-hand combat—and then the battle changes. After the devil has launched all his fiery slings and arrows—after he has hurled his horrible spears and slashed at you with his evil sword—after he has done his worst from a distance—without effect, if you have, in fact, put on the full armor God has issued you—after all that, the devil will keep coming.

෧ঌ෯

The devil wants to get his dirty hands on you. The devil wants to get in close to you, hoping to overcome the advantage of your divine protective armor. And so, you will wrestle with the devil up close and very personal—face-to-face—close enough to see the enemy as he goes for your throat—close enough to smell him and feel him as he tries to destroy you.

You must defend yourself or be defeated. And you *can* defend yourself, when you are in the clutches of the devil. But you will need even more than God's standard-issue spiritual armor then.

To know what you will need, you have to understand what you're struggling against. Our pew Bibles say, *"our struggle,"* but Paul actually wrote, *"we wrestle."* He chose that word intentionally because, in Paul's world, wrestling was a contest that involved cunning, trickery and deception, as well as strength. The point was to take your opponent down, in whatever way you could. Conversely, while wrestling in vicious, hand-to-hand combat, staying firmly on your feet was crucial.

The devil will wrestle with you—*is* wrestling with you. And when you wrestle with the devil, you're dealing with a "no holds barred" opponent because the devil will give no quarter and show no mercy, though he will beg for it constantly to throw you off balance.

And should you be confused by his cunning or distracted by his deceit—should you trust his promises or sympathize with his distress—he will turn these traits to his advantage and come back at you all the harder.

You have to know these *"wiles of the devil."* The Greek word for "wiles" is "μεθοδος,"—*"methodos,"* or "methods," and this word, too, implies the negative: his are cunning and tricky "methods." You have to be able to recognize the methods the devil uses to push or pull you down. His methods are fear and pessimism, shame and pride, jealousy and envy and hurt feelings and the like. You must not let him put these holds on you; you must block them whenever you feel them being used.

ॐक

But most of all, you must *"be strong"*—or better yet, *"be* **strengthened***."* It doesn't matter how strong *you* are—this is not a physical contest of blood and flesh. Paul means that you must "be continuously empowered" by the strength of the Lord by planting your life in the Lord Whose grace and power are sufficient for all our needs.[105]

The devil you are wrestling with is stronger than you, but he is nothing compared to the strength that is *in* you because you are in Christ Jesus.[106]

So, stand your ground in Christ against the devil's vicious and cunning assaults. After all, you hold the high ground—the high ground Jesus has already won[107]—and commands you to hold. As you wrestle with the devil, look where you are. You are standing on a hill called Calvary. So fight on—fully armored, completely aware and divinely strengthened. Wrestle that deceptive devil—and win![108]

ॐक

---

[105] 2 Corinthians 12:9.
[106] 1 John 4:4.
[107] 1 Corinthians 15:56-58.
[108] James 4:7.

From the Letter to the Philippians

Philippians 1:12-18 NRSV

^{12} *I want you to know, beloved, that what has happened to me has actually helped to spread the gospel,* ^{13} *so that it has become known throughout the whole imperial guard and to everyone else that my imprisonment is for Christ;* ^{14} *and most of the brothers and sisters, having been made confident in the Lord by my imprisonment, dare to speak the word with greater boldness and without fear.*

^{15} *Some proclaim Christ from envy and rivalry, but others from goodwill.* ^{16} *These proclaim Christ out of love, knowing that I have been put here for the defense of the gospel;* ^{17} *the others proclaim Christ out of selfish ambition, not sincerely but intending to increase my suffering in my imprisonment.* ^{18} *What does it matter? Just this, that Christ is proclaimed in every way, whether out of false motives or true; and in that I rejoice....*

అను

14.

Imprisonment for Christ

Philippians 1:12-18 NRSV

"I want you to know, brethren, that what has happened to me has really served to advance the gospel."

How do you explain what has happened to you?

Imprisonment—a condition that demands interpretation—what does this experience "mean"? For Paul, it was the difference between "human reason" and "divine purpose." Paul was in prison, but the gospel is not

At every opportunity, Paul concerned himself with the defense and vindication of the gospel. Paul was a single-minded man—he viewed everything through the lens of the gospel. The meaning of everything was determined by its relationship to the gospel. It was his universal point of reference—his "true north."

His imprisonment was not a disaster or a defeat. It was not a proof of the failure or falsehood of the gospel—no matter what anybody said or thought—because it wasn't that to him.

It wasn't what he would have chosen if it had been up to him. He made it clear he would rather be with all the people who loved and supported him.

But Paul saw his life through the eyes of Christ, and from that perspective, this imprisonment was an incredible evangelistic opportunity that would never have become available if he hadn't been where he was.

What Roman guard was going to notice or pay attention to Paul unless he had been ordered not to take his eyes off Paul (his prisoner) for hours at a time? Paul was stuck in prison, but the guard—and his reliefs—were stuck with Paul.

And Paul was making the most of the opportunity. He was not sitting there moping in silence. He was "advancing the gospel," one guard at a time—all day, every day. What did Paul want most? To advance the gospel. What was Paul doing in prison? Advancing the gospel.

Life was good.

తు•త

"It has become known throughout the…guard and to all the rest that my imprisonment is for Christ."

"My imprisonment is for Christ."

The Roman authorities put him in prison because he was telling people about this guy Jesus. In that sense, his imprisonment was for Christ. Christ—or Paul's loyalty to Christ, and his determination to talk about and promote Christ—was Paul's "crime." It was the human reason they put him in prison.

But his non-stop talking about the gospel while he was in prison made his imprisonment *"for Christ"* in another way. It served Christ. Advancing the gospel had been made the divine purpose for his imprisonment.

Paul told the story of Christ. He demonstrated the character of Christ. He lived by faith in Christ, through the grace of Christ, with the Spirit of Christ, conscious of the presence of Christ, excited to be doing the work of Christ

"It has become known throughout the…guard and to all the rest."

"To all the rest"—who is that? Everybody the guards are talking to—family, friends, supervisors, strangers in the marketplace.

"It has become known…"

These guys weren't Christians—not all of them—or even most of them, probably. But they were so fascinated by this weird guy in prison who wasn't bothered by his imprisonment—this guy who was excited and happy about being able to talk about his Jesus to these guys who couldn't avoid listening to everything he had to say because they have to make sure he didn't get away...

They are so fascinated that they couldn't *not* tell other people about Paul and what he was telling them. Paul was not going anywhere, but the gospel sure was, and Paul knew it. Paul knew that the gospel was known because his situation was known.

"I am put here for the defense of the gospel...." And Paul didn't seem the least bit upset about the "putting." He just went about the business for which he had been put there.

स•स

"Most of the brethren have been made confident in the Lord because of my imprisonment, and are much more bold to speak the word of God without fear."

What happens to you can and will affect other people. How you respond to what happens to you will affect them even more.

Most of *"the brethren"* were not bolder because Paul was in prison; they were energized by what his imprisonment meant to him and what he was doing with it. They caught his vision, and with that vision they caught his confidence and his courage and his passion and his energy.

Now here's a question: Were "the brethren" Paul was talking about in the prison with him—or outside, in the free world? Whether the brethren were the other prisoners or Christians outside the prison, they experienced a freedom of the heart and mind by seeing Paul's reaction to his imprisonment that they did not have before, inside or outside the prison.

Paul said they were *"made confident in the Lord,"* not in Paul. Paul's experience, and his understanding of the meaning and opportunity of his experience, led the Christians around him to focus their attention and faith on the Lord and experience for themselves a greater confidence—not in a servant of the Master, but in the Master Himself, Who provides all the spiritual strength and confidence Paul demonstrated in his confinement.

≈

"Envy and rivalry…partisanship… to afflict me in my imprisonment."

Not everybody was excited about Paul's excitement about the gospel and the opportunities prison gave him to defend and advance it. He had his detractors. He had people who were intentionally trying to mess with him—*"to afflict"* him. And they called themselves Christians, too, if you can believe it.

Even when you're spreading the gospel like a crazy man, prison is no picnic. Spreading the gospel gives prison a whole new and better meaning, but people trying to "stick it to you," especially if they're doing it because you're sharing the good news of Jesus, could break your heart or your spirit.

But Paul had already won—or let Jesus win—the battle with his ego—his pride. It wasn't about him, so what other people were doing about him, or to him, really didn't matter for him. What mattered to him was what people were doing for the gospel—whatever the human reason—because he knew the divine purpose was being served.

≈

…in every way…Christ is proclaimed…and in that I rejoice.

≈

15.

What It All Means

Philippians 1:21-30 ESV

²¹ For to me, to live is Christ and to die is gain. ²² If I am to go on living in the body, this will mean fruitful labor for me. Yet what shall I choose? I do not know! ²³ I am torn between the two: I desire to depart and be with Christ, which is better by far; ²⁴ but it is more necessary for you that I remain in the body. ²⁵ Convinced of this, I know that I will remain, and I will continue with all of you for your progress and joy in the faith, ²⁶ so that through my being with you again your boasting in Christ Jesus will abound on account of me.

²⁷ Whatever happens, conduct yourselves in a manner worthy of the gospel of Christ. Then, whether I come and see you or only hear about you in my absence, I will know that you stand firm in the one Spirit, striving together as one for the faith of the gospel ²⁸ without being frightened in any way by those who oppose you. This is a sign to them that they will be destroyed, but that you will be saved—and that by God. ²⁹ For it has been granted to you on behalf of Christ not only to believe in him, but also to suffer for him, ³⁰ since you are going through the same struggle you saw I had, and now hear that I still have.

❧

Ever come in on the tail end of a conversation and think, "*That* must have been interesting!"?

That's what you got with Paul this morning: *"For to me, to live is Christ and to die is gain."* You know where he goes with it in the verses that follow, but you didn't get a chance to hear where he was coming from.

Where Paul was coming from, geographically, was Rome, from a house he had rented, or more likely, had been loaned, probably by someone in the Roman church. He was getting to know the house well, because he never left it. Paul was under house arrest, chained up—perhaps to a rotating series of Roman soldiers—while he awaited a trial that would determine whether he would live or die...

...which brings us to where Paul was coming from, philosophically. Knowing that someone is going to make a decision sometime soon about whether you will be allowed to live or sentenced to die can get you thinking about life and death—and talking about it with people who are close to you—who know the fate you're facing. No church is closer to Paul than the one in Philippi—they are sending support to him in his prison[109]—all the way to Rome. And from his prison, Paul talks to them about the meaning of life—and death: his and theirs—and ours.

The part of this conversation we missed is Paul saying, *"I eagerly expect and hope...that Christ will be exalted in my body, whether by life or by death."*[110]

❦

The ultimate earthly reality is life and death—the existence of life and the absence of it. You and I believe, in faith and by revelation, that there is infinitely more, both here on earth and in heaven, both now and for all eternity.[111] If we are right, the meaning of life and death is wrapped up in that greater reality.

---

[109] Philippians 4:10-19.
[110] Philippians 1:20, ESV.
[111] John 3:16; 10:10.

But more and more of our neighbors here on Planet Earth do not believe what we believe. They do not share our faith or accept the revelation that shapes our understanding of life and death. For more and more people, the apparent reality of the "here and now" is all the reality there is: There is life and death and that's all. We live—and then we die.

If this is the extent of reality, life and death have no meaning. There is no higher purpose—no intelligent design—no reason that life began and no reason that it should continue. There is no value to life, except for the fluke that some forms of life have awareness of pain and pleasure and the desire to experience the one and avoid the other as long as the awareness exists.

The concepts of right and wrong in this perspective are merely the complex responses to the individual or collective impulses related to pleasure and pain. The purpose of life is to keep on living with as much pleasure and as little pain as possible. Death has no purpose, and therefore, no meaning.

As the old song said,

> "If that's all there is, my friend,
> then let's keep dancing.
> Let's break out the booze
> and have a ball—
> if that's all there is."[112]

❧

But to Paul, chained up and waiting for the word that will free him or finish his life on earth, that's not all there is—to life—or death. To Paul, whose life has been filled with so much pain that could easily have been avoided if avoiding pain had been its purpose—whose life has shunned so much of the pleasures other lives have sought—life and death are something totally different.

---

[112] Jerry Leiber and Mike Stoller, "Is That's All There Is," (released) 1969.

To Paul: life? Christ! Death? Gain! Paul found faith when he received a revelation from beyond this reality.[113] He learned that life is not a fluke; it is fiat. Paul encountered the One Who did not come into existence by accident[114]—the One Who always existed[115] and spoke out in the infinite, eternal reality beyond our severely restricted human perception of reality, calling all other life into existence.[116] And because this conscious, intentional Creator[117]— this Master Designer of all other reality[118]—caused life, life has meaning beyond the experience—beyond the impulsive desires— of those who have been caused to live.[119]

The meaning of life is what the Creator of life means for it to be.[120] The meaning of created life resides not in the preference of the creature but in the purpose of the Creator.[121]

And if life, as created, is limited—in this realm of reality—if the Creator Who could easily extend life indefinitely here has not chosen to do so[122]—then there is a reason for that as well. Death now has a meaning as truly and as profoundly as life does.[123] Both life and death have divine meaning.

ৰ৵৶

And so, back to Paul, chained up in a prison, considering his circumstances and sharing his conclusions with his friends in Philippi. Paul wonders, "Will I live or die? What am I going to do?"

But he's not wondering in the way you would think. Paul is not concerned with whether the Roman authorities will let him live or

---

[113] Acts 9:3-6.
[114] John 1:1.
[115] John 1:2.
[116] John 1:3.
[117] Genesis 1.
[118] Psalm 145:1-6.
[119] Psalm 8:3-6.
[120] Acts 17:28.
[121] Genesis 1:26-28.
[122] Genesis 6:3; Psalm 90:10.
[123] Romans 3:23.

execute him. He is not concerned with how to prolong his life and maximize its pleasures. He is not concerned to avoid the pain of physical punishment or violent death.

Paul is working on different questions: "How do I exalt Jesus Christ in my life as long as I have it?" and "How do I honor Christ in my death when it comes?"

What is the meaning of life?

The short answer is, "Christ."

From the day the resurrected Christ revealed Himself to Paul, every day for Paul was lived in Christ, for Christ, with Christ, by Christ. Christ was the purpose for Paul's life. Paul was single-minded in his obsession to know Christ and to make Him known.[124] Paul had discovered, up close and personal, that Jesus Christ, the Incarnation of the Creator God into humanity, is the ultimate expression of what human life means to God.[125]

Christ reveals what we mean to God[126]—and what God meant in giving us life[127]—and what God means to do with our lives.[128] Christ defines for Paul the meaning of his imprisonment, the meaning of all the painful things in his life,[129] the meaning of all the pleasures he sacrificed.[130]

"For to me, to live is Christ." "Everything I do in my life—every day I live—is for and about Christ. While I sit around here chained to this centurion, it's about Christ. While I wait to go to court, my life is about Christ. *To live is Christ."*

If Paul is right, to grow up is Christ. To fall in love and get married is Christ. To raise a family and pursue a career is Christ. To face hardships and disappointments is Christ. To grow old and know sickness and sorrow is Christ.

---

[124] 1 Corinthians 2:2; Philippians 3:7-11.
[125] Ephesians 4:13-15.
[126] John 3:16.
[127] Galatians 4:4-5; Titus 2:11-14.
[128] Romans 8:19-23.
[129] Romans 5:3; 8:18.
[130] Philippians 3:8.

What does life mean? It means nothing—or Christ. If there is no God, life has no meaning. If God exists, *"to live is Christ."*

&⋅&

And death? Without God, death has no purpose—no meaning. It's just the end of an accidental and meaningless life. For those in pain: Death is the final pleasure. For those still able to enjoy some pleasure: It is an inconvenient pain.

But for Paul, *"to die is gain."* The God Who gives life meaning gives death meaning as well, because live and death are not the opposite realities this world assumes them to be. Death is not the end of the life that God has created. It is but the point of transition from the limited life of this reality to the limitless life that we have been created to live in God's infinite eternity.[131]

How can Paul be so sure of this "gain" through death? Another of those little wrinkles in the original Greek wording provides a clue: Paul actually says, *"to **have died** is gain."* In the book of Galatians, he wrote, *"I have been crucified with Christ and I no longer live..."*[132] Paul has already died—with Christ.

Paul explained to the Roman Christians what God had revealed to him about this death business: *"...Christ being raised from the dead will never die again; death no longer has dominion over him.... So you also must consider yourselves dead to sin and alive to God in Christ Jesus. ... if Christ is in you, although your bodies are dead because of sin, your spirits are alive because of righteousness."*[133]

Now, Paul will acknowledge to the Philippians a little later, *"Not that I have already obtained all this,"* (meaning he has not yet experienced the physical resurrection Jesus has), *"but I press on to take hold of that for which Christ Jesus took hold of me.... I press on toward the goal to win the prize for which God has called me heavenward in Christ*

---

[131] John 5:24; Luke 23:39-43; Romans 6:4.
[132] Galatians 2:20, RSV.
[133] Romans 6:9, 11; 8:10, RSV.

Jesus."[134] In other words, "to have died in Christ is to have gained everything God has promised about the life He created in me."

That's what death means: life forever…

❧

…which sounds a lot better than life here, as the world commonly understands it. So why doesn't Paul choose death—God's peaceful portal into eternal bliss—while he weighs his options? No more suffering. No more sorrow.

But Paul is not living the kind of life that ends with death. Remember: *"For to me, to live is Christ."* And it's the same life in Christ, whether it's before or after Paul's physical death. Sitting in Rome, studying his chains, Paul remembers dying with Christ so that Christ would live in him. *"The life I now live in the body, I live by faith in the Son of God, who loved me and gave himself for me."*[135]

And the Christ Who now lives in Paul lives in him *for* these Philippian Christians, just as He lived in the world for all of us. And just as Christ gave Himself up for Paul, Christ in Paul is giving Paul back to them for their benefit—and, ultimately, for ours, too.

The revelation Paul received on the Damascus Road[136] has become our revelation. And the faith Paul placed in the risen Christ has become our faith. We, like Paul, have been crucified with Christ and Christ lives in us, too, so that for *us* to live is Christ and to die is gain.

What does it all mean?

Let's let Paul have the last word on that: *"If we live, we live to the Lord; and if we die, we die to the Lord. So, whether we live or die, we belong to the Lord."*[137]

❧

---

[134] Romans 3:12, 14, NIV.
[135] Galatians 2:20, NIV.
[136] Acts 9:3-6.
[137] Romans 14:8, NIV.

Philippians 2:1-13 NRSV

¹ *If then there is any encouragement in Christ, any consolation from love, any sharing in the Spirit, any compassion and sympathy,* ² *make my joy complete: be of the same mind, having the same love, being in full accord and of one mind.* ³ *Do nothing from selfish ambition or conceit, but in humility regard others as better than yourselves.* ⁴ *Let each of you look not to your own interests, but to the interests of others.* ⁵ *Let the same mind be in you that was in Christ Jesus,*

> ⁶ *who, though he was in the form of God,*
> *did not regard equality with God*
> *as something to be exploited,*
> ⁷ *but emptied himself,*
> *taking the form of a slave,*
> *being born in human likeness.*
> *And being found in human form,*
> ⁸ *he humbled himself*
> *and became obedient*
> *to the point of death—*
> *even death on a cross.*
> ⁹ *Therefore God also highly exalted him*
> *and gave him the name*
> *that is above every name,*
> ¹⁰ *so that at the name of Jesus*
> *every knee should bend,*
> *in heaven and on earth and under the earth,*
> ¹¹ *and every tongue should confess*
> *that Jesus Christ is Lord,*
> *to the glory of God the Father.*

¹² *Therefore, my beloved, just as you have always obeyed me, not only in my presence, but much more now in my absence, work out your own salvation with fear and trembling;* ¹³ *for it is God who is at work in you, enabling you both to will and to work for his good pleasure.*

ॐॐ

16.

Off the Same Sheet of Music

Philippians 2:1-13 NRSV

A few moments ago, we sang a hymn. At the end of the service, we will sing another. Though these hymns are perhaps not the most familiar, we announce the number of each so that you will be encouraged to sing them and not some other hymn you may know better and like more.

As the saying goes, we "sing off the same sheet of music." To do otherwise—to let each of you sing whatever song you might feel like singing just then—would create chaos and a very literal and audible disharmony. "Doing your own thing" is not the best way to approach congregational singing.

"Singing off the same sheet of music" has become a common figure of speech because the idea has even wider applicability. The need for harmony and unity extends to all aspects of our experience as a church family. But we tend to be less willing to take direction in other areas of our corporate lives as Christians than we are when singing hymns together.

That's why Paul is so determined to "announce the number" for Christians in those other areas of life, too. That's what he's doing when he tells the Christians in Philippi, *"Let the same mind be in you that was in Christ Jesus."* "Everybody needs to be singing 'the Jesus song.'"

And how does that go?

৯-৩

It begins with unity. That's the basic melody. Jesus was united with God the Father in attitude and intent,[138] and this unity of mind enabled Jesus to want what His Heavenly Father wanted[139] and to do what He was directed to do.[140]

You avoid wrong notes by avoiding selfish ambition or conceit. They are simply not a part of the key in which this song is sung. Every time you sound a note of personal desire or ego, it will not fit the chord. It will be flat. You will need to raise it to a higher level—to the level of humility, in fact—where you choose to view those around you as better than yourself. Humility, as it turns out, is the moral and spiritual equivalent of perfect pitch.

The lyrics of this Jesus song are interesting and out of the ordinary. Ordinarily, we tend to sing: "Me, me, me, me!" And, although we can sing that song loud and long, it's actually rather boring—and remarkably hard to harmonize with anything else.

On the other hand, "You and you and you and you" can be sung in an infinite number of variations and harmonizes extremely well with what Jesus sang.

Is the idea of everybody singing off the same sheet of music a silly way of expressing the need for unity in the church? After all, rumor has it that some people don't even open the hymnal when the number is announced (and not because they know every song by heart). Is it fair or realistic to talk about singing "the Jesus song" together?

Well, you ought to know that Bible scholars are convinced that part of what was read from Philippians today was an early hymn

---

[138] John 10:30.
[139] John 4:34.
[140] John 5:17, 19.

about Christ—a hymn that Paul quoted. Verses six through 11 contain a hymn these first Christians would have known and sung many times before Paul used it to illustrate his point about their need to be in harmony as followers of Christ. His message was in the music, even then: Think like Jesus. Live like Jesus.

How does the hymn go? He emptied Himself—humbled Himself—became obedient unto death.

Paul has "announced the number." This is "the Jesus song."

Let's all sing it together.

る◦ゟ

Philippians 2:2-11 ESV

[2] ... *complete my joy by being of the same mind, having the same love, being in full accord and of one mind.* [3] *Do nothing from selfish ambition or conceit, but in humility count others more significant than yourselves.* [4] *Let each of you look not only to his own interests, but also to the interests of others.* [5] *Have this mind among yourselves, which is yours in Christ Jesus* [6] *who, though he was in the form of God, did not count equality with God a thing to be grasped,* [7] *but emptied himself, by taking the form of a servant, being born in the likeness of men.* [8] *And being found in human form, he humbled himself by becoming obedient to the point of death, even death on a cross.* [9] *Therefore God has highly exalted him and bestowed on him the name that is above every name,* [10] *so that at the name of Jesus every knee should bow, in heaven and on earth and under the earth,* [11] *and every tongue confess that Jesus Christ is Lord, to the glory of God the Father.*

❧

17.

The Empty God

Philippians 2:2-11 ESV

The Bible begins with a profound and primal truth: *"In the beginning, God created the heavens and the earth. And the earth was without form, and void"*[141]—or "empty."

The Gospel of John begins with an equally profound revelation: *"In the beginning was the Word, and the Word was with God, and the Word was God.... And the Word was made flesh, and dwelt among us...."*[142]

Creation and New Creation.

And Paul adds to the revelation of this New Creation in the second chapter of his Philippian letter. And if he had put it in the literary form of the beginning verses of Genesis and John, he might have said, "In the new beginning, God designated a Savior from the heavens for the earth, and the Savior was God, and this time, it was the God Who would save the world Who was without form and void"—a simple, single human cell, to begin with—placed, by the will of God and nothing else, in a virgin's womb.

---

[141] Genesis 1:1-2, KJV.
[142] John 1:1, 14, KJV.

Christ Jesus, Paul says, *"...was in the form of God...."* He was the equal of God. In Colossians, Paul calls Christ, *"the image of...God..."* in Whom *"all the fullness of God was pleased to dwell."*[143]

We're talking about God here. And yet we're talking about God emptying Himself of everything divine, so that He could become everything human—except sin.[144]

And so, for a lifetime—a single human lifetime, or less, since this particular Life was cut off in its prime—God stopped being God (as we conceive of God) and became a Man. For a fleeting moment—an instant in the infinite expanse of eternity—the divine Word—God—became flesh and dwelled among us—as one of us.

The God Who could do anything with His infinite power,[145] could not do this one thing—achieve the salvation—the redemption—of a fallen humanity formed by Him in His image[146] and de-formed by sin—even with all the power He possessed. This defeat of sin in mankind could only be accomplished through weakness. The Deliverer of sinful humanity could only defeat sin by dying at the hand of sin—and dying for sin—the sin in others— and dying as sin—though He never committed a sin.[147] Someone had to die for sin, and yet not *deserve* to die for sin. In other words, God had to die for sin—no one else could.

And yet, how can the God Who is the Source and Sustainer of all life die? And how can the God Who is perfect holiness—perfect purity—become sin? And how can anyone ever be saved from sin if God cannot—or does not—do the saving?

And so, though it was impossible, God did what had to be done. And to do this impossible thing, God emptied Himself of all the power and wisdom and knowledge and authority and status

---

[143] Colossians 1:15-20, ESV.
[144] Hebrews 4:15.
[145] Mark 10:27.
[146] Genesis 1:26-27.
[147] 2 Corinthians 5:21.

and splendor that were His, by right and by might. He gave them up.

There is a line in a popular praise song that says,

> "He gave His life;
> what more could He give?"[148]

And the true answer is, "Quite a lot more." Infinitely more, according to Paul. Jesus Christ gave up His human life. But in becoming Jesus Christ, God could—and did—give up His omnipotence, His omniscience, His omnipresence. He gave up everything about Himself that was divine except the bare and unalterable fact that He *was* divine.

"Oh, how He loved you and me?" If you think all your Savior did was suffer and die for you, you don't know the half of it!

When young David went to fight Goliath to save God's people, Saul, his king, tried to deck David out in his own royal armor. But the shepherd boy took it all off and set it aside, taking only a slingshot and a few river rocks to do battle with the giant.[149]

And when God came to fight the decisive battle with the greater giant, sin, He took off and set aside, not merely the elements of royal armor, but the entirety of His divine defenses, to be born as a helpless Son of David and go into His greatest battle with not even a slingshot or a stone in hand.

The old folks used to sing in the hymn "Rock of Ages,"

> "Nothing in my hand I bring,
> simply to Thy Cross I cling."[150]

And so brought the God Who emptied Himself of His every defense for us: nothing in His hands but the nails that pierced them and pinned Him on His cross.

On that cross, dying as the only Sacrifice that would work to pay for our sins and free us from sin's condemnation, God in Christ had to be God-less—He had to be "man-without-God"—

---

[148] Kurt Kaiser, "Oh, How He Loves You and Me," 1975.

[149] 1 Samuel 17:1-51.

[150] Augustus Montague Toplady, "Rock of Ages," 1763.

or it wouldn't work; it wouldn't be real. And so, upon the Cross, dying as the Man Who had successfully emptied Himself of His rightful divinity, our Christ, our Messiah, our Savior, would cry out in His human agony what so many men and women before Him had cried,

> *"My God, my God, why have you forsaken me?*
> *Why are you so far from saving me…?"*[151]

And the answer was that the God Who had become Man was too close to saving the world for that great victory to be aborted by God saving Himself instead. Christ had chosen to do God's will when it could not be done by God *as God.* And in His dying, as a Man alone, unaided by God, Jesus Christ accomplished God's great purpose in emptying Himself to become man.

Paul said, *"Christ Jesus…emptied himself, by taking the form of a servant, being born in the likeness of men. And being found in human form, he humbled himself by becoming obedient to the point of death, even death on a cross."*

❧⸻❦

But once He had died—really died—like all humans do and God cannot—*then*, all the infinite, divine power of God could be brought to bear again—for things like raising Jesus from the dead and restoring Him to His rightful place in the Godhead—and restoring to Him all that was rightly His that He had set aside to become our Savior.

God accomplished what He did in Jesus—*as* Jesus—because He emptied Himself *of* Himself. He saw the solution to sin in sacrifice of Self. He took the form of a servant. Though Lord of lords and King of kings, *"he humbled himself and became obedient."*

And Paul tells the Church, *"Have this mind among yourselves that is yours in Christ Jesus…."*

---

[151] Psalm 22:1, ESV.

And the writer of Hebrews says, *"...let us also lay aside every weight... looking to Jesus, the founder and perfecter of our faith, who... endured the cross...and is seated at the right hand of the throne of God."*[152]

So many people in this world are like floundering swimmers, adrift and drowning in an endless sea of sin? Are you one of them?

You cannot save yourself by "taking control" of the situation. The situation is hopeless. Your life is lost if someone doesn't come and help.

And there is help. There is a Lifeguard swimming out to you, but He says, "Let go and let Me save you. Stop grasping to hold onto *Me*—and let *Me* hold onto *you*. If you will let go, nothing will pry you out of My hands."[153]

The Lifesaving God says, "I emptied Myself of everything to save you. Empty yourself of everything to live the life I saved you for. Empty yourself so that I may fill you with the glory and power and wisdom and love I filled Jesus with after He emptied Himself of all the divine attributes that were rightly and eternally His.

God says, *"My strength is made perfect in [your] weakness."*[154] His strength *is* made perfect in your weakness—as it was in the weakness of His Son, Jesus. God says, "Empty yourself of everything you have grasped in this world trying to keep yourself afloat, so that I may fill you with everything I created you to have to live abundantly and forever with the One Who emptied Himself *of* all—and is now exalted *above* all."

"Have this mind in you that was in Christ Jesus."

❧

---

152 Hebrews 12:1-2, ESV.
153 John 10:28-29.
154 2 Corinthians 12:9, KJV.

Philippians 2:5-11 NRSV

5 *Let the same mind be in you*
that was in Christ Jesus,
6 *who, though he was in the form of God,*
did not regard equality with God
as something to be exploited,
7 *but emptied himself,*
taking the form of a slave,
being born in human likeness.
And being found in human form,
8 *he humbled himself*
and became obedient to the point of death—
even death on a cross.
9 *Therefore God also highly exalted him*
and gave him the name
that is above every name,
10 *so that at the name of Jesus*
every knee should bend,
in heaven and on earth and under the earth,
11 *and every tongue should confess*
that Jesus Christ is Lord,
to the glory of God the Father.'

ॐ

18.

Imagine a Light

Philippians 2:5-11 NRSV

Imagine, if you will, a light—brighter than a candle or a lamp or a lighthouse—brighter than the sun—in fact, brighter than all the suns in the universe combined—brighter by far than any other light could ever be. Imagine a light that has always been there—always the same—never different, never divided, never diminished.

And then, see this light—this Light—singular and unchanging since "forever before time"—at one particular moment in time—become two Lights—a part that has not changed, remaining exactly as it has always been—and another part that remains Light, but dims to the point that you can see now, in addition to its light, a form that you had not—and could not have—seen before: a human form—as familiar and unremarkably human as the Light had been unique and unfathomable in its brilliance just an instant before.

And now, this Light in human form moves—no longer located at the center of the universe where the ultimate and eternal Light has always been—always shined. The human Light leaves the great and unequalled Light of which It has always been (and even now continues to be) a part, and comes down—"down" because every direction from the great Light is "down." The human Light comes down to a pitifully small speck of dirt and rock and water spinning along insignificantly through the far recesses of space.

And the Light in human form becomes but one of the countless human forms populating this place. This Light—He— lives a human life alongside every other human. All are human, but He alone is human *and* Light. None of the humans see the Light in Him at first—they only see the human form, which is what the Light wants them to see at first. But soon, they see that this Human is different; He is more. Because He is the Light, He is different. Because He is the Light, He is more.

Some see the Light within this Human and respond to what they see as any consciousness should respond to ultimate Light: by approaching It with joy. And they are en-Light-ened.

Others—most of the humans, in fact—see the light in Him as something that needs to be put out. And they proceed to take away His human life in an attempt to extinguish the Light within Him.

And what is perhaps as remarkable as the fact that He is human and Light is that He allows them to take His human life. He does what no sane human wants to do—give up His life—because this was the purpose for which the Light separated in the first place.

The Light took on human form—became truly human—to overcome the darkness at the core of the lives of the humans who populated the puny little planet of rock and dirt and water spinning off in the recesses of the universe that belongs, with everything in it, to the one great Light at the center of, and, at the same time, above, the universe.

The Light in human form allowed the other humans to do whatever they wished to do to destroy His human life. And by doing so, the Light fulfilled the purpose for which It—He— became human. The human life ended and the Light that was in human form went out.

☙❧

But the end of Light and life that was intended and seemingly accomplished could not be sustained—because it was not the intention of the great ultimate Light that remained. The Light that forms and sustains these destroyers of life—and their planet—and the universe in which that planet with them on it moves—restored the Light and the human form in Which It dwelled. And the part of the Light that had become human returned to, and became again One with, the ultimate, eternal Light.

But now, if you could see the Light that is, and always will be, the Light beyond our ability to comprehend, you would discern still the human form—once so remarkable—but now transformed into the form of humanity like no other. And you would see, as well, other human forms gathered around that One that is human yet Light, and you would see them infused with that same Light and transformed by It.

And though you cannot see them, you may be able to look around you here—on this puny planet of dirt and water and rock— and see humans in whom that Light shines. Look around you as you go about your business each day. Look around you as you gather to pray in this place. Look, perhaps, even in the mirror.

Wherever a knee bows to the Light or a tongue confesses Its power and glory on this planet, the Light dwells—shines within that human form. The knee bows and the tongue confesses because the Light became human and came to humans and died as a human and has been raised up to life and Light again by the Light that lives forever. You who bow and confess will live in His Light and be transformed by His Light.

You will see what you can only now imagine.

৯৯৯

Philippians 3:4b-14 NRSV

⁴ *If anyone else has reason to be confident in the flesh, I have more:*
⁵ *circumcised on the eighth day, a member of the people of Israel, of the tribe of
Benjamin, a Hebrew born of Hebrews; as to the law, a Pharisee;* ⁶ *as to zeal,
a persecutor of the church; as to righteousness under the law, blameless.*

⁷ *Yet whatever gains I had, these I have come to regard as loss because of
Christ.* ⁸ *More than that, I regard everything as loss because of the surpassing
value of knowing Christ Jesus my Lord. For his sake I have suffered the loss
of all things, and I regard them as rubbish, in order that I may gain Christ*
⁹ *and be found in him, not having a righteousness of my own that comes from
the law, but one that comes through faith in Christ, the righteousness from God
based on faith.* ¹⁰ *I want to know Christ and the power of his resurrection and
the sharing of his sufferings by becoming like him in his death,* ¹¹ *if somehow I
may attain the resurrection from the dead.*

¹² *Not that I have already obtained this or have already reached the goal;
but I press on to make it my own, because Christ Jesus has made me his own.*
¹³ *Beloved, I do not consider that I have made it my own; but this one thing I
do: forgetting what lies behind and straining forward to what lies ahead,* ¹⁴ *I
press on toward the goal for the prize of the heavenly call of God in Christ
Jesus.*

&~&

19.

That I May

Philippians 3:4b-14 NRSV

Have you ever wanted something so badly that nothing else mattered? Most of the time, when you want something that much, it turns out badly, because most of what we want that badly is bad.

But not always. Jesus told a parable about a man who found a pearl of such great value that Jesus approved of his selling everything he had so he could buy it.[155]

In this passage from Philippians, Paul rattles off an impressive list of assets and accomplishments—and then immediately says that everything important he is or has done in his life has been a waste of time—or worse—compared to something he now wants very, very much.

Everything he had amassed in a lifetime of dedicated, diligent effort turned out to be extremely impressive—and ultimately meaningless to Paul when he compared it to something else that had come to matter to him more than anything else.

What is Paul playing at here? What's his game?

It's the game of life, actually. People refer to the game of life rather flippantly. But it's a pretty good analogy. Many people have

---

155 Matthew 13:45-46.

compared life to this game or that. You can play all kinds of games in life. You can play more than one. But suppose you've been playing the wrong game?

Human life is interesting in that people can play many different games—at the same time—on the same playing field: this old planet earth. You can play—or try to play—any game or games you choose. Some games are more common and popular than others. The more people who play a particular game, the greater the pressure you will feel to play it, too.

৵৹৵

But suppose all games are not the same. Suppose one game is not as good as another. Suppose they're not all of equal value, just because people want to play them. Suppose there is an official Scorekeeper for the one game in life that really matters—THE Game of Life.

And suppose you discover—at the end of your life or very near it—that yours wasn't the game that really matters—and that whatever score you amassed playing it doesn't matter, either—doesn't even count. The other game—the only game that really matters in the end—was going on all around you the whole time—and you have been awarded a score by the Scorekeeper in that game—even though you weren't playing it.

What's the point in achieving a great score in the game you're playing if you're playing the wrong game? What's the value of all your points if, in the only game whose score is going to be counted, you never got on the board?

If you discover one day you've been playing the wrong game all your life—even if you've played it well—you need to do what Paul did. Paul had been playing the game called "How Good Can I Be" all his life. He was a "scratch" player. He won tournaments.

And then, he discovered he was playing the wrong game. In a blinding flash, he came to realize the only game that mattered was "Knowing Christ." That's the only score that counts. And in that moment, all the career statistics and single day records Paul had amassed became worthless to him—not to everyone else who still played "How Good Can I Be" every day, but to Paul. To him, those "points" were nothing because they didn't count. They were worse than nothing, because he had wasted so much time and effort playing that game, and amassing those points, when he could have been playing the other game—the one that mattered.

ᕙ•ᕗ

Listen to what he wrote: *"Whatever gain I had, I counted as loss— for the sake of Christ. Indeed, I count everything as loss—because of the surpassing worth of knowing Christ Jesus my Lord."* Paul stopped playing the wrong game as soon as he realized what the game of life really is: "Knowing Christ."

"I gave up the old game and I don't miss it." That's what he means when he says: *"I suffered the loss of all things and count them* (even now) *as refuse* (something to be thrown out or flushed down the drain)." Paul is playing a different game now. He has sacrificed everything that used to be important in the old game so that he can become a winner in the new one.

And he has a game plan. He let everything else go in life. He refused to play any other games, and he took this rather obsessive approach for a reason—or better yet, a group of related reasons. The list is clearest in the Revised Standard Version, where Paul says, "I have done 'this'…so that I may do 'that.'"

And what are Paul's "that I mays"?

ᕙ•ᕗ

Paul says, *"…that I may gain Christ and be found in him."* Paul gave up everything else because he found the pearl of greatest price.[156] You cannot take Christ,[157] but you can receive Him.[158] Whatever it

---

[156] Matthew 13:45-46.
[157] John 15:16.
[158] John 1:12.

135

took, Paul was determined to "gain Christ." It took putting everything else with whatever goodness or value in the "loss" column. This was not Paul "finding a place for Christ" in his life. It was God finding a place "in Christ" for Paul's life. This is the fundamental difference between winning and losing the game of life.

Paul wanted to be so connected with Christ that you couldn't see Paul without seeing the influence of Christ over him and the activity of Christ in him. Paul wanted to be so attached to Christ that no one would have any doubt as to what game Paul was playing.

"He used to be so good at the 'How Good Can I Be' game, but he's exclusively a 'Knowing Christ' player these days."

That's why he gave up every other game people play. The "Knowing Christ" game is the only one that matters, and you can't play it using your own natural abilities. You can't play it with your head.

❦

In the long run, it's not what you know—it's Who you know and how you know Him.[159] Paul gives up everything—materially, socially, culturally and psychologically—in order to know Christ in an experiential, intimate way.

Paul understands that "Knowing Christ" requires that he be a friend of Christ rather than a fan.[160] Paul wants the experience of a genuine relationship with Christ—and what he wants to experience is the power Christ's Resurrection has already released into the lives of His friends and followers.

And like soldiers who go to war with a great leader, Paul knows that the only way to know Christ as intimately as he needs to and wants to is to make the sacrifices and endure the suffering that

---

[159] 1 Corinthians 2:2.
[160] John 15:14-15.

warriors share in combat with the enemy.[161] He measures his success in knowing Christ, not by what he gets, but by what he is enabled to give up.

The game is played in the arena of the power Christ's Resurrection immediately unleashed.[162] But the victors in this game are rewarded with the ultimate experience: the resurrection of the body. And don't let Paul's humility fool you. He knows that playing this game in the power of Christ's Resurrection means that the eternal, physical and spiritual Resurrection will one day be his, too.[163]

In the game of life, it matters very much whether you win or lose,[164] and winning is all about how and whether you play the right game the right way. Paul can show you the way.

As with certain other games of near-religious dimensions,[165] a few lessons can really "improve your game."

☙❧

---

[161] 2 Timothy 2:3-4.
[162] Revelation 20:6.
[163] Romans 6:5.
[164] Matthew 25:31-34, 41.
[165] This sermon was preached in a church in Pinehurst, North Carolina, where many people are very avid golfers.

Philippians 3:4b-14 ESV

[4] *If anyone else thinks he has reason for confidence in the flesh, I have more:* [5] *circumcised on the eighth day, of the people of Israel, of the tribe of Benjamin, a Hebrew of Hebrews; as to the law, a Pharisee;* [6] *as to zeal, a persecutor of the church; as to righteousness under the law, blameless.* [7] *But whatever gain I had, I counted as loss for the sake of Christ.* [8] *Indeed, I count everything as loss because of the surpassing worth of knowing Christ Jesus my Lord. For his sake I have suffered the loss of all things and count them as rubbish, in order that I may gain Christ* [9] *and be found in him, not having a righteousness of my own that comes from the law, but that which comes through faith in Christ, the righteousness from God that depends on faith—* [10] *that I may know him and the power of his resurrection, and may share his sufferings, becoming like him in his death,* [11] *that by any means possible I may attain the resurrection from the dead.*

[12] *Not that I have already obtained this or am already perfect, but I press on to make it my own, because Christ Jesus has made me his own.* [13] *Brothers, I do not consider that I have made it my own. But one thing I do: forgetting what lies behind and straining forward to what lies ahead,* [14] *I press on toward the goal for the prize of the upward call of God in Christ Jesus.*

৵~৶

20.

Total Loss—Greater Gain

Philippians 3:4b-14 ESV

I know it's the Bible, but it sounds like one of those commercials for a brokerage firm, or a report on the economy: "Everything I thought was going to turn a profit I'm putting in the loss column," Paul said.

Now, I'm not an expert when it comes to reading a balance sheet, but I know "the bottom line" is important. So what's the bottom line when everything you invested in is a total loss?

In the Bible, it can be better than you think.

The Apostle Paul held stock in an old established firm known as Judaism Incorporated. It specialized in religious and moral applications and had a long and respectable track record. Paul had carefully managed that portfolio, part of which he had inherited from his stock holder parents, and some he had later obtained by his own investment. He had impressive holdings.

But more recently, Paul had altered his investment strategy based on a new evaluation of his assets. He had literally stumbled across a new "start up" not long after its Initial Public Offering (IPO). And to everyone's shock and amazement, including his own, Paul's entire perspective on investment changed, radically, in the process.

It's not so much that he divested himself of his old portfolio; he just ignored it. He began devoting every waking minute to expanding his holdings in this new start up. He joined the company, such as it was, and became its most effective spokesman. He became a man obsessed, not so much with the company—though he did seem to be setting up branches everywhere he went—but with the Founder of the company, a remarkable Individual Who captivated Paul from the first moment they met.[166]

Before they actually met, Paul had done everything he could to sabotage the start-up,[167] sensing that it was a threat to Judaism Inc., and Paul's significant investment there. And he was right—at least in the sense that the new company, Jesus Christ and Associates—would be competing directly for stock holders and would force a serious reassessment of the ability of Paul's old firm to fulfill its investor's expectations.

And after Paul met the Founder of this new enterprise, Jesus Christ, he realized that his old portfolio didn't matter. They weren't bad stocks. In fact, they were better than anything else on the market until this new company came along. But Paul saw pretty quickly that they just weren't going to achieve his investment goals; Judaism Limited, for all its fine qualities and wonderful products, wasn't going to get Paul where he wanted to go.[168]

The only thing that would or could was the return on what Paul received from the Founder of the new company. And here's the funny part: Paul didn't actually buy a single share of the stock of Jesus Christ and Associates. The Founder wasn't selling it—He was giving it away.[169]

Jesus Christ, the Founder of this new rag-tag but revolutionary company, was giving away what the recipients like Paul soon realized were incredibly valuable assets—things that were not

---

[166] Acts 9:3-6.
[167] Acts 8:3; 9:1-2.
[168] Romans 7:7-24.
[169] Ephesians 2:8-9.

available anywhere else, from anybody else. Members of the new company experienced spectacular profit merely from accepting the Founder's invitation to join the company and work alongside Him. As long as they were with Him, the Founder just kept adding to their portfolios.

And that's why Paul could say, "I came to realize that any investments I hold in any other stocks are absolutely worthless for meeting my ultimate investment goal. What the Founder of the company provides free of charge is all I need, and worth far more than the time I spend with the Founder and everything I experience in the service of His company."

You see, the Founder of Jesus Christ and Associates showed Paul that Paul's best investment strategy was to copy the Founder's investment strategy. That's not an unheard-of strategy, even today. There are many people who just do what some investment guru does—to the degree that their lesser resources allow. The key is: Who do you decide to follow?

When Paul picked Jesus Christ as his investment guide, he picked Someone Who had already shown Himself willing to invest everything He had—every bit of His personal capital—to create Jesus Christ and Associates, the company Paul joined. Paul conveniently summarized that investment strategy in the second chapter of Philippians: Jesus Christ divested Himself of every other asset He possessed so that He could, in humility and obedience to God, form this company, and by doing so, realize the greatest return on investment in all of human history.[170]

And what about Paul's return on investment? What assets did he realize because of his commitment to Jesus Christ and Associates? The company terminology for these unique and priceless assets is δύναμις—"*dunamis*" and κοινωνία—"*koinonia*." "*Dunamis*" is the word behind "dynamo" and "dynamic." It means unequalled "power." "*Koinonia*" is "sharing"—"fellowship."

---

[170] Philippians 2:5-9.

Paul devotes himself to Jesus Christ and Associates and the Founder provides Paul and every other stock holder—free of charge—the *"dunamis"*—the power—of His Resurrection and the *"koinonia"*—the intimate fellowship—of His suffering.

That *dunamis* and *koinonia* that God the Father supplied Jesus Christ are the resources that enabled the founding and the preservation of the company to which Paul and now all of us belong. We are the return on the Founder's investment. And His power in us and His fellowship with us are the profit beside which everything else of value appears worthless.

As he writes to the Philippians, Paul is going over the books—conducting an audit of his spiritual portfolio. And he's got some miscalculations to correct. Above the column with "circumcision, Israel, Benjamin, and Hebrew"—above the words "Pharisee, zealous and faultless"—Paul carefully strikes through the title "Assets" and writes "Total Loss."

And out beside that list, he begins to write another one with a hand now shaking with excitement: *"Knowing Christ—and the power of his resurrection and the fellowship of sharing in his sufferings—and having a righteousness that comes from God through faith...."* He pauses for a moment, considering what he has written, and then above it he writes, "The Greatest Gain—in this World—and the Next."

☙❧

Hosea 5:15—6:6 ESV

[God said to Hosea:]

> **5** *¹⁵* *"I will return again to my place,*
> *until they acknowledge their guilt and seek my face,*
> *and in their distress earnestly seek me."*

[The people said:]

> **6** *¹* *"Come, let us return to the* LORD*;*
> *for he has torn us, that he may heal us;*
> *he has struck us down, and he will bind us up.*
> *² After two days he will revive us;*
> *on the third day he will raise us up,*
> *that we may live before him.*
> *³ Let us know; let us press on to know the* LORD*;*
> *his going out is sure as the dawn;*
> *he will come to us as the showers,*
> *as the spring rains that water the earth."*

[God said to the people:]

> *⁴ "What shall I do with you, O Ephraim?*
> *What shall I do with you, O Judah?*
> *Your love is like a morning cloud,*
> *like the dew that goes early away."*

[God said to Hosea:]

> *⁵ "Therefore I have hewn them by the prophets;*
> *I have slain them by the words of my mouth,*
> *and my judgment goes forth as the light.*
> *⁶ For I desire steadfast love and not sacrifice,*
> *the knowledge of God rather than burnt offerings."*

ॐ

Philippians 3:7-11 ESV

[7] But whatever gain I had, I counted as loss for the sake of Christ.

[8] Indeed, I count everything as loss because of the surpassing worth of knowing Christ Jesus my Lord. For his sake I have suffered the loss of all things and count them as rubbish, in order that I may gain Christ [9] and be found in him, not having a righteousness of my own that comes from the law, but that which comes through faith in Christ, the righteousness from God that depends on faith— [10] that I may know him and the power of his resurrection, and may share his sufferings, becoming like him in his death, [11] that by any means possible I may attain the resurrection from the dead.

જી્જી

21.

It's Who You Know

Hosea 5:15—6:6; Philippians 3:7-11 ESV

The old saying goes, "It's not *what* you know; it's *who* you know." Whatever you're trying to accomplish, it implies, your associations are more important than your abilities.

Better to depend on your interpersonal network than your individual merits.

And cynical as it sounds, it's often right. And it's absolutely right regarding matters of ultimate reality. When it comes to heaven, hell and the living of this life, Who you know matters more than anything else.

Unfortunately, more and more people today not only don't know the right "Who." They don't even know the "what" that will help them meet the "Who" they need to know more than anybody else.

The "Who" they need to know—we all need to know—is God. That's what the prophets and the apostles were saying in Bible times, and that truth hasn't changed. The Prophet Hosea knew that too many people knew too many other gods at a time when his country was coming apart and needing all the holy help it could get.

The people in charge of the country were putting their faith in all the wrong "whos," hoping that hasty alliances with other countries, large and small, would keep them safe from threats they could not overcome themselves. And the people themselves spent their time celebrating all the other gods, assuming that, when it comes to things religious, "the more, the merrier."

This seemed like a good plan because they had forgotten Who got them where they were in the first place—the divine Who Who had also been giving them all the good things they had enjoyed ever since. They no longer knew their own God, and what was happening all around them was the proof.

God said, through Hosea,

> *"There is no faithfulness or steadfast love,*
> *and no knowledge of God in the land....*
> *My people are destroyed for lack of knowledge."*[171]

And Hosea saw the similarity between Israel's unfaithfulness to her God and that of his own despicable wife to him. His wife didn't have a clue or a care about loving her husband with true covenant devotion.[172] And God's people didn't treat their Lord any better.

Oh, when their political and economic situation "went south," the people sang the old religious songs:

> *"Come, let us return to the Lord...*
> *he will heal us...he will bind us up...*
> *he will revive us and raise us up...*
> *he will come to us for sure."*

Sounds like all the people who showed up in all the churches after 9/11 shook everybody up so bad. "Come, let us return to the Lord—for a couple of weeks, until we feel better—for a little while, until we see if anything else bad is going to happen."

But God is not impressed with puny gestures of religious practice. You see, knowing God, which is what God wants from

---

[171] Hosea 4:1, 6, ESV.
[172] Hosea 1—3.

us, isn't just coming to church once in a while, (though coming to church is something I would not discourage as a rule). Knowing God is not putting money in the plate—even in sacrificial sums— (though the ministries of the church do require financial support).

What God wants is true, God-like love and the kind of "knowing" that comes from an interactive, personal relationship that is far deeper than detached theological thinking and religious rituals performed by rote. Drawing on Hosea's marriage imagery, God says to His unfaithful people,

> *"I will betroth you to me*
> *forever.*
> *I will betroth you to me*
> *in righteousness and in justice,*
> *in steadfast love and in mercy.*
> *I will betroth you to me*
> *in faithfulness.*
> *And you shall know the Lord."*[173]

Why is "knowing God" so absolutely vital?

God is the One Who punishes us when we are sinful—the One Who causes us to reap what we sow. God is too dangerous *not* to know!

And God is the One—the only One—Who can heal us and save us when we are, otherwise, totally lost and completely destroyed. God is the only One Who can do for us what must ultimately be done for us.

God knows us, certainly. He knew us before we were conceived[174] and has had complete and perfect knowledge of us every moment of our lives.[175] God knows us infinitely better than we know ourselves.[176]

---

[173] Hosea 2:19-20, ESV.
[174] Psalm 139:13; Jeremiah 1:5.
[175] Matthew 10:29-31.
[176] Psalm 39:4.

But how are we to know God in the way that He wants us to know Him?

We can only know what He is willing for us to know—what He chooses to reveal of Himself to us.[177] Of that, God will cause us, help us, to know as much as we are willing to know—all that we seek to know about Him.[178] Read your Bible. Pray. Listen to sermons. Share in fellowship and perform ministry. These activities will help, but they are not the goal.

God wants you to know Him directly—personally—and He will not be satisfied until you do. To make that possible, God *"emptied himself ... taking the form of a servant, being born in the likeness of men."*[179] And so, it is possible to know God now in a way that Hosea hardly could have conceived.

Please understand, knowing *about* God is not *knowing* God. The Apostle Paul knew all about God. Everything his Bible said about God, Paul had studied carefully and committed to memory, so he could do exactly what God wanted Him to do—except Paul didn't know God well enough to know that knowing *about* God wasn't what God wanted from him at all. Paul thought it was all about *"what* you know."

And then, Paul met God in the person of Jesus Christ and, in Christ, he finally got to know God the way God wants to be known. It's not *what* you know, it's *Who* you know. And when Paul realized that he could, finally, truly know God, that's all he ever wanted from then on.

He called it *"the surpassing worth of knowing Christ Jesus my Lord."*

To know someone, you have to meet him, spend time with him, communicate with him, observe him in many situations, come to trust him. You become close, understanding his character, values and goals. You dedicate yourself to your part of the relationship.

---

[177] Deuteronomy 29:29.

[178] Isaiah 55:6; James 1:5-6.

[179] Philippians 2:7, ESV.

A relationship as demanding as the Prophet Hosea saw marriage to be—and "knowing God" to be—is actually more demanding than going through a routine of church rituals. But then again, you can't get what you truly need from God by trying to butter Him up a little with a few visits to His house[180] and a few coins in His coffers.[181] That's the kind of love that dissolves like the dew at dawn, and God surely knows the difference.

Paul found that he came to know God best by sharing in the sufferings of Christ. That's a love that doesn't melt away like the morning mist. And in that faithfulness that would not let go of the God Who would not let go of him,[182] Paul found that he was being formed into the likeness of Christ, that he had come to know the God Who was Christ so well that, with the Holy Spirit's help, he could imitate Christ in his own life—and death.

৯৽৽৾

We began by talking about what a failing country needed to do to get back on track and save itself from the coming catastrophe its own faithlessness had caused. The simple truth is that, at any point in history, it will take a people who come to realize that the secret to social and spiritual salvation lies not in *what* they know, but in *Who* they know, people willing to know that Who—and love that Who—and submit themselves in humility and repentance to that Who, with the total dedication He demands.

So let us conclude with the critical question: "Do *you*...know *Who*?

৯৽৽৾

---

[180] Amos 5:21.
[181] Amos 4:4-5.
[182] Romans 8:38-39.

149

Philippians 4:4-7 NRSV

⁴ Rejoice in the Lord always; again I will say, Rejoice. ⁵ Let your gentleness be known to everyone. The Lord is near. ⁶ Do not worry about anything, but in everything by prayer and supplication with thanksgiving let your requests be made known to God. ⁷ And the peace of God, which surpasses all understanding, will guard your hearts and your minds in Christ Jesus.

৶৶

22.

Responding to Rough Times

Philippians 4:4-7 NRSV

In his weekly radio broadcast called *A Prairie Home Companion*,[183] Garrison Keillor begins his popular monologue by saying, "It's been a quiet week in my hometown, Lake Wobegon."

Well, it's been anything but quiet everywhere else this week. Stock markets around the world have taken up sky-diving. Politicians in Washington have been startled awake and resolved to take quick and drastic action—a scary prospect in its own right. And you and I have seen our assets evaporate like steam from a boiling pot.

All of a sudden, everything seems to be coming unglued, and worst of all—we think—is the fact that we don't really know how bad it's going to get. Everybody's concerned. Some people are terrified. What do you do in a situation like this?

The Bible says, "Rejoice."

I'm not making this up. The lectionary readings for this Sunday include the passage from Philippians where Paul says, *"Rejoice in the Lord always. And again I will say rejoice."*

---

[183] *A Prairie Home Companion* was broadcast from 1974 until 2016.

Sometimes the readings for a Sunday seem tailor-made for our circumstances. Sometimes they seem "180-out."

Rejoice?

With what's going on?

Maybe this is one of those weeks where these pre-chosen Bible readings don't really apply to our specific situation.

❦

Or maybe they do.

Remember that things are not exactly "peachy" for Paul or the Philippians as he writes this letter. Paul's in prison and his readers are struggling with persecution, internal conflict and economic hardships of their own.

For us, this passage is usually about how wonderful everything is. It's our permission to celebrate our good fortune.

That's not why Paul tells the Philippian Christians to rejoice.

Paul tells them—*orders* them—to rejoice always, as a continuous, ongoing behavior and attitude. But the rejoicing is not related to their human circumstances, which are subject to change at any time, and were never very good at the best of times.

They are to *"rejoice in the Lord...."* Whatever their circumstances, what has happened to them through and in Jesus Christ is enough to justify non-stop celebration.

The ultimate "circumstance" is your relationship with Jesus Christ. If it is the saving, redeeming, sustaining relationship of grace through faith, it trumps everything in this world for importance.

To people with that relationship, Paul can say, "Have no anxiety about anything else." The biggest circumstance of all is taken care of, and all the others will find their proper place under it.

Whatever the human circumstance, rejoice. After all, you know two very important things as a Christian. One is that the Lord is at hand. Your sovereign God and personal Savior is present and available to you. To paraphrase one *not*-so-old spiritual: "[Your] Lord is near [you] all the time…[your] Lord is near [you] all the time."[184]

Another reason to rejoice in times like these is the promise Paul provides that we incorporate into every service. At the conclusion of this service, you will receive a benediction based on this assurance that the peace of God, which passes all understanding, will keep your hearts and minds in Christ Jesus.

☙❧

I don't understand much about markets and economics, but I do understand that whatever happens in them, God is still sovereign and able to provide for me in ways that are also beyond my understanding. In fact, the word Paul uses for "keep" is a military term, and our pew Bibles pick that sense up, translating it as "guard." God "stands the watch" over you and me. God is the Sentry Who protects us in dangerous times and territory.

Are we at risk?

All the time, in this life.

Are we guarded, protected from, and secured against, these earthly risks?

Absolutely, and all the time—in Christ Jesus—by God Himself.

"But these are scary times!"

Yes, but rather than responding with anxiety (which serves no productive purpose and may actually make the situation worse), rejoice in the spiritual resources that can never be devalued or lost, and take the anxieties and fears you do have to God in prayer, asking for what you need, while thanking God for what He has already provided, and is even now providing.

Rough times?

Rejoice.

---

[184] Barbara Fowler Gaultney, "My Lord is Near Me All the Time," 1960.

Rejoice in the Lord.
Rejoice in the Lord always.
Rejoice.

ﮮﮧ

From the Letter to the Colossians

Colossians 1:15-23 ESV

¹⁵ *He is the image of the invisible God, the firstborn of all creation.* ¹⁶ *For by him all things were created, in heaven and on earth, visible and invisible, whether thrones or dominions or rulers or authorities—all things were created through him and for him.* ¹⁷ *And he is before all things, and in him all things hold together.* ¹⁸ *And he is the head of the body, the church. He is the beginning, the firstborn from the dead, that in everything he might be preeminent.* ¹⁹ *For in him all the fullness of God was pleased to dwell,* ²⁰ *and through him to reconcile to himself all things, whether on earth or in heaven, making peace by the blood of his cross.*

²¹ *And you, who once were alienated and hostile in mind, doing evil deeds,* ²² *he has now reconciled in his body of flesh by his death, in order to present you holy and blameless and above reproach before him,* ²³ *if indeed you continue in the faith, stable and steadfast, not shifting from the hope of the gospel that you heard, which has been proclaimed in all creation under heaven, and of which I, Paul, became a minister.*

ॐ

23.

Who is this Guy?

Colossians 1:15-23 ESV

Well, put on your thinking caps; today, it gets "technical."

"Jesus loves me, this I know,"[185] but today, we're not talking about "Gentle Jesus, meek and mild."[186] Today, we confront "The Cosmic Christ."[187]

You know how, when you go to a planetarium, you can sit and look at the stars and they will show you where the constellations are and tell you mind-boggling things about our solar system and the galaxies beyond. You can sit there and look out into space.

Suppose there was a "time-atarium," a place where you could go and see all the way back to the beginning of time. There is such a thing, of course. It's called the Bible. From the first chapter of Genesis to the last chapter of Revelation, the Bible is the place you can go to find out about time—whether you want to see what happened at the instant when time came into existence,[188] or what the end of time will look like.[189]

---

185 Anna Bartlett Warner, "Jesus Loves Me," 1859.
186 Charles Wesley, "Gentle Jesus, Meek and Mild," 1742.
187 The title or partial title of a number of books.
188 Genesis 1:1-5.
189 Revelation 6:12-14; 21:1.

The Book of Colossians provides one of the most interesting exhibits in the "time-atarium." It takes you right back to the very beginning, just like Genesis 1 does. But where Genesis zooms in on what is happening here, Colossians goes the other way, and takes in the whole infinite scope of the Creation. Where Genesis focuses on the detailed results, Colossians looks at process and purpose—the technical side of Creation.

And if there is technology, you can reasonably assume a technician. A "result" reasonably suggests a "cause" behind it. Everything that happens—everything that has *ever* happened—has been caused-to-happen by something else—all the way back to the beginning.

Do the research, and you can figure out the cause—except in one particular case. How could it all begin unless there was a Beginner-of-it-all Who did not begin—Who just was?

Like I said: "It gets technical."

☜∙☞

How and why did it happen, this first "causing" of everything? Good thing you've got a "time-atarium" so you see what happened. The Genesis exhibit shows you that *"In the beginning, God created...."*[190] God is the Beginner Who did not begin—Who, unlike anything else, just (and always) *was*.

Another exhibit—the one in the first chapter of the Gospel of John—shows you that *with* God in the beginning—an actual *part* of God—was Something called *"the Word."*[191] When you look at the Word, you're looking at the knowledge, the know-how, the technical expertise of the Creator God, the Beginner of all things—that part of God that is able to cause things to be that do not exist—to cause things to have life that didn't (and couldn't) live otherwise.[192]

---

[190] Genesis 1:1, ESV.
[191] John 1:1-2.
[192] John 1:3-4.

And when the Beginner began everything, everything—without exception—was begun by this part of God called "the Word."

But when you look in Colossians, you see that this Word, this creative wisdom and power of God, is called other things, too: *"beloved Son of God"—"first-born of all creation"—"Christ."*

And you see more.

Not only is this awesome aspect of God the force and wisdom that caused the first "effect," and the process of cause-and-effect that would ensue from it, It—or He, if you will—is the Location where all of Creation was brought into existence, and the Destination to which all of Creation is going. He is the Purpose behind Creation—it has all been made for Him.

৯৫৩৯

Now, turn your "time-atarium" around. Look out into the end of time.

Everything is going *to* Him. Just as He decided and knew how to create all things, He will determine what will happen to everything when the cause-and-effect process of time is brought to a close.

Oh! And see something else: The creative power of God—the Word, the Son, the Christ—is not just the Cosmic Starter and the Cosmic Concluder, He is the timeless Cosmic Sustainer of Creation, He is that aspect of God that keeps every galaxy, every planet, every person, every speck of matter in existence existing throughout every moment during all the time He has chosen to provide. *"In him, all things hold together."*

Your biblical "time-atarium" will show you the beginning of time and the end of time, and it will let you look at a lot of time in between. It will show you the time when the Cosmic Christ became the Carpenter of Nazareth, when the un-caused infinite Power of Creation became a poor finite Creature caused by a miraculous conception and a common birth. For a time, the timeless Word of

159

Creation became the time-bound Worker of redemption. And He did the work of divine redemption through simple human words and sacrificial human deeds.

For a time, the Cosmic Christ was "gentle Jesus, meek and mild." For a time, the Son of God was the Man of Sorrows.[193] He wasn't much to look at—only *"the image of the invisible God."* He appeared to be an ordinary guy, but *"in him all the fullness of God was pleased to dwell."*

And speaking of the pleasure of God: Just as God brought everything into existence through this Christ Who, at a particular point in time, was born and lived as Jesus, God was also pleased to reconcile to Himself all things, in all Creation, through the human blood of this Jesus Who was still also the Christ as He died upon His Cross.

Jesus died, as people will do. But though Jesus was people—a Person—He was also by this time the Christ Who created all things at the beginning of time, and Who sustains all things throughout time, and Who awaits all things at the end of time.

ॐ॰ॐ

And so, guess what?

The death that comes in time to all people—to all of Creation—had a hard time holding the Source of life itself "down."

Look! The Firstborn of all Creation is also the Firstborn from the dead. The Cosmic Christ of Creation has now become and will remain forever the Jesus Christ of Redemption. The Technician of Creation turns out to be the Technician assigned to accomplish God's re-Creation as well. Don't underestimate this Guy.

And don't spend all your time at the "time-atarium" looking at the beginning of time or the end of time—or even at that time when Jesus Christ lived and died and rose again. You need to look at *your* time. *"You who were once estranged and hostile in mind, doing evil deeds...."*

---

[193] Isaiah 53:3.

There was a time when that was you—perhaps it still is. If it *is* your present, don't let it become your future, because you don't know how much time you have left.

If it is your past, praise God! Praise God—as long as your present is *"securely established and steadfast in the faith, without shifting from the hope promised by the gospel that you heard."* And don't tell me you "hope so," because your hope and the hope in Colossians are not the same thing at all.

Your hope may be wishful thinking, but the hope they're talking about is the warranty issued by the Technician on the work of Redemption He did for you. It's a guarantee that's not just "good as gold." It's infinitely better.

ॐ

If you were estranged from God in the past, hold on to that God-given guarantee of reconciliation in the present, because there is an incredible future before you. Sooner or later, your time here will be over. For creatures like us, the present all too quickly becomes the past.

But for creatures who have become like Christ Jesus—for people who become His Body—for you who are the Church—the future is a *time*less time that encroaches with grace upon the present. It is a time when this time-creating God—incarnated in a timeworn and now time-conquering Man— *"will present you holy and blameless and irreproachable"* to Himself for all time.

Sometimes, the technology of a thing is just too technical to understand. You watch the technician work and wonder what he's doing—how he gets the result he does. Sometimes, you just have to trust him.

You check his credentials, of course. You listen to referrals and consider his track record. And, in time, you come to realize that you can depend on an ability that is far beyond your own. You can trust the guy.

Today, it got technical. If your head hurts, I understand. If the concept of the Cosmic Christ is too complicated to get your mind around, that's okay. If looking back to the beginning of time—or forward to the end—is just too far for a Sunday morning service— if Creation and Consummation are too much, then do this: Just focus on Him Who is *"the image of the invisible God."*

And it's okay if all you see is "gentle Jesus meek and mild." The truth is: You could boil all the technical stuff down to this:

> "Jesus loves me,
> this I know,
> for my biblical 'time-atarium'
> shows me so."

❧❦

24.

Captivity of the Mind

Colossians 2:6-10 ESV

⁶ Therefore, as you received Christ Jesus the Lord, so walk in him, ⁷ rooted and built up in him and established in the faith, just as you were taught, abounding in thanksgiving.

⁸ See to it that no one takes you captive by philosophy and empty deceit, according to human tradition, according to the elemental spirits of the world, and not according to Christ. ⁹ For in him the whole fullness of deity dwells bodily, ¹⁰ and you have been filled in him, who is the head of all rule and authority.

∞⚬∞

The Thirteenth Amendment of the U.S. Constitution abolished slavery and involuntary servitude in America, except as punishment for crimes.[194] The Fourteenth Amendment prohibits depriving any person of life, liberty, or property, without due process of law.[195]

And yet, every day, countless people in this country are taken captive, young and old, rich and poor, strong and weak. Every day, people allow themselves to be taken captive by what the Apostle

---

[194] Ratified December 6, 1865.
[195] Ratified July 9, 1868.

Paul calls *"philosophy and empty deceit."* To be taken captive by philosophy and empty deceit suggests that we're not dealing with an "invasion of the body snatchers,"[196] but rather with an "invasion of mind snatchers."

Paul warned the Colossian Christians to be on their guard because there were people out there who were trying to get them to look at life and the world in ways that leave Jesus on the sideline. In the 1st Century, the world was filled with sure-fire ways to get ahead in life—to get past fate, or the mysterious forces of nature, or the control of the stars. There was always somebody who promised to let you in on the secret to getting over on all the other people who were always in the way of your success. It was "snake oil" for the mind.

And there's a sucker in every crowd, just gullible enough to fall for a lot of fast talk and fuzzy logic promising the moon or the secrets of the universe, or something that seems worth giving up your mental and moral freedom for. And for all our 21st Century sophistication, the risk of being taken captive by philosophy and empty deceit is greater now than ever. Now, the deceivers don't have to knock on your door or buttonhole you on the street. They wait patiently till you turn on your TV or computer, or get yourself comfortable in your seat in the theater or a classroom, or tune them in on your smart phone or other personal devise.

They don't even have to set or spring the trap themselves. They can deputize your favorite celebrities, powerful politicians, your mentors, classmates, family and friends. Now as then, the world is full of these empty and deceitful philosophies that capture your thinking and corrupt your life by coaxing you away from the real source of power and wisdom for life: Jesus Christ.

అ•త

---

[196] American science-fiction horror movies, *Invasion of the Body Snatchers*, 1956, 1978, 1993, 2007. In the last two remakes, the titles were changed to *Body Snatchers* and *The Invasion*, respectively.

"See to it that no one takes you captive," says Paul.

Let's break that down.

"See to it" means "pay attention"—know the risk and know that you *are* at risk. Know that there are people out there every day, committed to capturing your mind, corrupting your perspective and controlling your behavior by messing with your values and your beliefs.

"See to it..." Don't sit back, helpless and unaware. Take action. Do the things you need to do to avoid the traps set for you—or be able to defend yourself against the effort to ensnare you. Make it a priority—make a plan—enlist help. See to it that the con man with the con job doesn't con you.

"See to it that no one takes you captive." "No one" implies that there is "someone" who will take you captive, if he or she can. Consider who the people might be who are most likely to want to influence your thinking in a way that diminishes the influence of Jesus in your thinking.

Whoever that "someone" is, make that person "no one" in your life, so that he or she cannot have a chance to take you captive.

"Empty, deceitful philosophies." Paul is talking about ideas that are both unprofitable and untrue—yet still remarkably seductive. Otherwise, it would not be necessary to be on your guard. You're only tempted by something you would naturally want to do. A seductive idea must *seem* profitable. It must *sound* true—even though it's not.

How do you know if a philosophical system is false and flawed? How do you test an idea to see if it is true and substantial?

Paul says the empty, deceitful philosophies are *"according to human tradition, according to the elemental spirits of the world, and not according to Christ."*

There's a litmus test for you! That will refine out the dross and purify the gold.

If the idea is based on a system of logic that starts with the supremacy of human thinking or human desire, you can be pretty sure the whole structure will sooner or later "go south." If it sets up some person as the guru of some special, superior wisdom—watch out! Human tradition always ends up on the trash heap of history.

And *"the elemental spirits of the world"* haven't fared much better. Nobody knows for sure what Paul meant by that phrase—whether demons—the stars—the four "elements" (earth, water, fire and air) that everybody in that day thought everything in the world was made of—or what.

Paul's point was that if you think ultimate truth comes from the natural world, your world view is going to be as useless and wrongheaded as those philosophies celebrating human genius as the foundation for understanding all reality.

"The problem, simply put," says Paul, "is that any philosophy that does not come from Christ or concur with Christ cannot render an accurate reading of reality. Any philosophy that attempts to compete with Christ as the answer to all the questions of life will eventually collapse, or perhaps implode, because it lacks the substance to stand the test of time or survive the unavoidable consequences of godless systems."

Philosophies rooted in Christ, on the other hand, are neither empty nor deceitful. *"In Christ, the whole fullness of God dwells bodily,"* Paul says. Christ is *"the head of all rule and authority,"* Paul says. *"And you have been filled in him."*

৯৩

So far, this has all been very "philosophical," and if you are still awake, you may be thinking, "What is he talking about? Is there any practical application here?"

Let's look at some of the kinds of ideas being used to take people captive today that Paul would warn us about.

One of them might be called the "I deserve to be happy" philosophy.[197] Sometimes, it's even dressed up with some religious trappings as, "I know God wants me to be happy."

Either way, this is an empty and deceitful philosophy. The deceit is in believing that anyone *deserves* happiness—or that God is particularly concerned about human happiness, individually or collectively. Faithfulness, *yes!* But happiness? Not necessarily.

The philosophy is self-deceiving because people who embrace it are really saying, "I should be allowed to do whatever I want to do without suffering any negative consequences, because I think (or hope) doing what I want to do will make me happy," even though God has made it clear in His Word that it won't make Him happy—and probably won't make them happy for long, if at all, and also probably will make other people *un*-happy because they will get stuck with paying the bill for, or with cleaning up the mess from, an unsuccessful attempt to obtain a remarkably elusive happiness.

৯৶৽

Another philosophy capturing the minds of people is the one that says, "I can do immoral things because morality doesn't matter anymore."[198] The corollary is "Everybody's doing it, so it's okay for me to."

The truth is that there are basic, primal moral laws that are part of God's created, righteous order that, when violated, will always disturb that order—and always bring suffering in their wake. The fact that the violator may not suffer immediately or in full measure appropriate to the immorality of the act does not mean that no one suffers or that society will not suffer cascading short- and long-term ramifications of a complexity and magnitude that the violator could not imagine or calculate.

---

[197] Genesis 3:6.
[198] 1 Corinthians 6:12.

Every instance of private recreational drug use has contributed in a substantial way to a global web of horrific drug cartels that now rule vast regions of the world with incredible cruelty.

Every sexual liaison before or outside marriage makes all marriages more difficult to preserve and any marriage less likely to be undertaken in the first place—in both cases corrupting the social and moral incubator of the family and robbing boys and girls of the opportunity to be raised up as responsible men and women. The abortion industry flourishes because so many now believe sexual morality "no longer matters."

Every act of cheating or fraud or dishonesty in school or business diminished the character and capability of the guilty individual, and damages the productivity and trustworthiness of the institution, weakening public confidence and raising the level of cynicism in society that restricts everyone's opportunity to excel.

తూర్తి

And then there's the philosophy that would take you captive with its mantra: "The earth is the *state's*, and all that dwell therein."[199]

Again, here is a philosophy that is neither true nor profitable for people, yet remarkably seductive, especially for those who can maneuver themselves into positions of power in the state, and those who trust that human beings in positions of power will be as wise, or generous, or equitable in the distribution of the earth's and the citizenry's resources as God has been.

But those who are able to act like God often find it most difficult, in the end, to discern the difference between themselves and God. And those who did not create the world are often, finally, inadequate to administer it with sufficient understanding, love and grace to justify making any organization of people a substitute for God.

---

[199] See Psalm 24:1.

There are many other empty and deceitful philosophies capturing the minds of the unwary person in these days. Time does not permit us to identify and consider more. But there must be a way to see them for what they are and avoid the pitfalls they present.

Paul says, *"See that no one takes you captive."*

How do you do that?

Even before the warning, Paul provides the answer in a hodge-podge of images: *"...as you received Christ Jesus the Lord, so walk in him, rooted and built up in him and established in the faith, just as you were taught..."*

Stay the course of the faith you were taught.[200] Walk in the footsteps of Christ Whose light will keep you from stumbling[201] like those who walk in darkness do.[202] Christ is the true vine and you are the branches.[203] Be rooted solidly in Him for stability in turmoil[204] and sustenance in a dry season.[205] Be built up in Christ, withstanding storms like a house built on rock instead of sand.[206] Be established in Christ by abiding in His word, so that you will know the truth and the truth will make you free.[207]

These are things to see to, and if you do, no one will take you captive with those philosophies of empty deceit.

৵৽৶

---

[200] Acts 20:24.
[201] John 8:12.
[202] John 11:10.
[203] John 15:5.
[204] Ephesians 3:17-19.
[205] Psalm 63:1.
[206] Matthew 7:24-27.
[207] John 8:31-32.

From the First Letter to the Thessalonians

1 Thessalonians 2:9-13 ESV

⁹ For you remember, brothers, our labor and toil: we worked night and day, that we might not be a burden to any of you, while we proclaimed to you the gospel of God. ¹⁰ You are witnesses, and God also, how holy and righteous and blameless was our conduct toward you believers. ¹¹ For you know how, like a father with his children, ¹² we exhorted each one of you and encouraged you and charged you to walk in a manner worthy of God, who calls you into his own kingdom and glory.

¹³ And we also thank God constantly for this, that when you received the word of God, which you heard from us, you accepted it not as the word of men but as what it really is, the word of God, which is at work in you believers.

જ⊷ઓ

Matthew 23:1-12 ESV

¹ Then Jesus said to the crowds and to his disciples, ² "The scribes and the Pharisees sit on Moses' seat, ³ so do and observe whatever they tell you, but not the works they do. For they preach, but do not practice. ⁴ They tie up heavy burdens, hard to bear, and lay them on people's shoulders, but they themselves are not willing to move them with their finger.

⁵ They do all their deeds to be seen by others. For they make their phylacteries broad and their fringes long, ⁶ and they love the place of honor at feasts and the best seats in the synagogues ⁷ and greetings in the marketplaces and being called rabbi by others. ⁸ But you are not to be called rabbi, for you have one teacher, and you are all brothers. ⁹ And call no man your father on earth, for you have one Father, who is in heaven. ¹⁰ Neither be called instructors, for you have one instructor, the Christ. ¹¹ The greatest among you shall be your servant.

¹² "Whoever exalts himself will be humbled, and whoever humbles himself will be exalted."

જ⊷ઓ

25.

A Lesson in Leadership

1 Thessalonians 2:9-13; Matthew 23:1-12 ESV

If you go browsing in a bookstore, somewhere in the non-fiction area you will find a section on "Leadership." In a small store, it may only be a shelf. In a large store, you may be confronted with an entire aisle on the subject, with dozens and dozens of books offering up the insights and advice of business, industry and government giants.

What you probably won't find in the leadership section, but should, is the Bible. Nowhere is there deeper insight or better advice on leadership than that found in the pages of scripture—as we shall see today.

Lessons in leadership would not be important for most of us, except for one thing: We are Christians, and every Christian is called to be a leader.[208] Your Leader, Christ, has made it very clear that everyone who follows Him—every Christian—is to be leading others. You are to be leading people to Christ. You are to be leading people into His Church. You are to be leading your fellow Christians, as Paul put it in the epistle reading today, *"to walk in a manner worthy of God."*

---

[208] Matthew 28:19-20.

We ask you to wear a name tag every Sunday. (Some who have special responsibilities in the service wear more than one.)

We could write "Christian Leader" under every name and we wouldn't be wrong—if you are a Christian. Christ, our Leader, has appointed every one of us—every disciple—to a position of leadership in the Church.

∾

"But I'm not a leader!"

You are if He says you are. You have been appointed a leader by Jesus Himself—and what is more—He has equipped you for the job: He has given you the Holy Spirit to empower you. What you lack in gifts and abilities, energy and experience, the Holy Spirit makes up.

You have been given the Bible, containing more practical insight and advice about leadership than all the other books ever written on the subject combined. In the Bible, the giants of the faith instruct you in leadership: Moses and Joshua, David and Daniel, Ezra and Nehemiah, Peter and Paul and Jesus Himself.

Look! Your Leader has made you a leader and He has equipped you for the job. You can lead, and Christ expects you to.

Of course, there is a difference between being a leader and being "in charge." In my time in the military, I observed many young men and women who wanted desperately to be "in charge" so they could lead. It generally worked the other way around. Those who demonstrated they could lead were eventually put in charge.

The truth is that you can be a superb leader and not be in charge of anything. To be called and equipped to lead as a Christian does not mean that you are necessarily called or equipped to be in charge of anything, whether denomination, church, class or committee. It does mean that wherever you are in this fellowship, with whatever gifts you do have,[209] you are to exercise leadership in the Body of Christ to further the work of His kingdom.[210]

In recent months, the political class in this country has been yammering over whether somebody who is in charge should forego the authority of that position to "lead from behind."

They'll never settle that one. And for most of us, that's a non-issue because most people will almost always be leading from behind or, at best, from beside. That's where we are. And leaders lead from where they are.

But *how* are you to lead as a Christian?

৯৯

Time for a lesson in leadership.

There are actually two lessons today: one from Jesus and one from Paul. Both offer examples, and Christians are to lead, in part at least, by example.

The example Jesus presents is negative on the whole: "Look at this," He says to His disciples. "Look, but do not copy." Leadership, according to Jesus, requires both preaching and practicing. This doesn't mean that you need to sign up to give the sermon one Sunday. But it does mean that Christian leadership— your leadership as a Christian—is not to be only about behavior. There are things you are to say, as well as things you are to do, if you are to be the leader Christ intends for you to be.

Christ shared some insight and advice about leadership when He criticized the religious leaders of His day. He wasn't after them for what they were saying, but for *not* doing what they were telling other people to do. And, to be fair, He also noted that they *were*, in some cases, doing things godly leaders should *not* be doing, regardless of what they were saying.

They were certainly in charge, but they were not leading properly.

---

[209] Romans 12:6-8.
[210] Ephesians 4:11-13.

175

To summarize the critique Jesus offered:

- Practice what you preach.
- Don't make it harder on people than it has to be to be obedient to God.
- Don't show off.
- Don't cultivate a personal fan club.
- Lead with genuine humility.

For Jesus, true leadership—both His leadership and the leadership He requires of His followers—is servant leadership: *"The greatest among you shall be your servant."*

And He was.

Jesus was, by far, the greatest among us. He fed the multitudes[211] and calmed the seas[212] and healed the sick.[213] But He also strapped on a towel to wash dirty feet[214] and then strapped on a cross to wash away our sins;[215] He did the work of the ultimate servant. And because He was our Servant, amazing as that is, we, too, are to be servants—servants leading.

❧

But how? How are you to be the leaders Christ has called and equipped you to be?

How do you do it?

The answer is: "Preach and practice—practice and preach."

Paul reminded the Christians in Thessalonica what he and others had said and done as their leaders. "Remember, we came alongside you and led you from there. We did not make it harder for you to be Christians; we did not lord our leadership over you. We shared the Christian life with you.

"What did we do?

---

211 John 6:1-13.
212 Mark 4:35-39.
213 Matthew 4:24.
214 John 13:2-5.
215 Titus 3:3-7.

"We took care of ourselves as best we could. We lived with you and showed you, in our behavior, holy, righteous and blameless lives. We practiced our faith so openly, consistently and committedly, that you never had to wonder if we really meant what we said to you about the gospel of Jesus Christ; you saw the truth in our lives every time you saw us."

That's what Christian leaders do to lead. When you live your life in holiness and righteousness, leaving no opportunity for anyone to challenge your dedication to Christ and His gospel, you have positioned yourself to be the effective Christian leader Christ has called you to be. And once you have established the practice of Christianity as your way of life, you are ready to "preach" the gospel persuasively, whatever words you use.

❧

And how did Paul preach to his fellow Christians?

He spoke encouragement to them. He spoke comfort. And he challenged them like a father with his beloved children to grow up in the faith and behave themselves in ways that bring honor and glory to God. Paul modeled his leadership on the leadership of Jesus, so that those he led to Jesus could do the same.

In this congregation, there are encouragers. Sitting among us today are holy comforters.

You are disciples of Jesus Christ who have given your lives to Him and then received them back from Him filled with His Spirit and guided by His Word, in order that you might be the leaders of the community of faith He has called us all to be, transforming lives in and beyond this fellowship, not by your own abilities, but by the miraculous gifts of God given to you as the equipment of leadership.

Every Christian—every one of you—is a leader in the kingdom of God. Every one of you is called and equipped to be the servant of salvation, leading those around you by your life and your testimony, loving those you lead like Christ loves them—and you.

This fellowship does not exist because two men were willing to preach for you.[216] It has not flourished because of the commitment and expertise of a few talented and dedicated souls. It will not become what God intends for it to be merely by the work and prayers of those in charge.

Every one of you has led this church forward. Every one of you is leading by word and deed, large or small. Every one of you is called to lead. Every one of you is equipped to lead. Every one of you as a Christian is a leader. God has seen to that.

You lead your leaders by your encouragement. You lead those who are burdened with your comfort. You lead the tempted by your dedication to holy and righteous living. You lead the cynical and doubting by your blameless example. You lead the tired and dispirited, if there are any, by your confidence and enthusiasm—in and for Christ, first—and because of that, in and for this fellowship.

Whether here and now, or somewhere else during the week, your every word—your every deed—is leadership—Christian leadership—Christ using you to move His Church in the direction He intends to take it.

Who's the leader?

If you're looking up here or around the room, don't bother.

Look in the mirror.

It's you!

☜☞

---

[216] When this particular church, Trinity Christian Fellowship, was established, the membership called me and another retired Navy chaplain to serve as co-pastors. We alternated preaching and worship leader responsibilities each week.

26.

Children of the Day

1 Thessalonians 5:1-11 ESV

[1] Now concerning the times and the seasons, brothers, you have no need to have anything written to you. [2] For you yourselves are fully aware that the day of the Lord will come like a thief in the night. [3] While people are saying, "There is peace and security," then sudden destruction will come upon them as labor pains come upon a pregnant woman, and they will not escape. [4] But you are not in darkness, brothers, for that day to surprise you like a thief. [5] For you are all children of light, children of the day. We are not of the night or of the darkness. [6] So then let us not sleep, as others do, but let us keep awake and be sober. [7] For those who sleep, sleep at night, and those who get drunk, are drunk at night. [8] But since we belong to the day, let us be sober, having put on the breastplate of faith and love, and for a helmet the hope of salvation. [9] For God has not destined us for wrath, but to obtain salvation through our Lord Jesus Christ, [10] who died for us so that whether we are awake or asleep we might live with him. [11] Therefore encourage one another and build one another up, just as you are doing.

❧

Paul has just started a new church in the Greek city of Thessalonica, one of many he's gotten up and running along the trade routes of the Roman Empire. And like a lot of new

Christians, the Thessalonians have some questions. And like a lot of Christians, new and old, one of the things they're curious about is when Jesus is coming back to raise the dead and bring the world to an end.

After all, you don't want to tie your capital up in any long-term investments if you're not going to be around to collect the profits. And at the same time, if this great "Day of the Lord's Return" is coming anytime soon, you may be able to put off some of those chores you really hate to do long enough that you'll never have to do them at all.

But Paul isn't much help: "I shouldn't have to write you about this. You know very well," he says, *"that the day of the Lord will come like a thief in the night."* Even Jesus said He didn't know when He was coming back. Nobody but God the Father knows when.[217]

☙❧

But we do know *how*.

Like a thief in the night: suddenly and without warning. And if you're not prepared, you lose. Like labor pains: one minute, nothing; and the next minute, "Uh-oh," it's "time," and here we go. If your suitcase isn't already packed, too bad.

On the other hand, if you knew it was coming and got ready, it's the thief in the night who's going to be frustrated.[218] If you're properly prepared, the trip to the hospital is a cinch, day or night. And you should be ready, because labor pains are a normal part of pregnancies, and thieves often go thieving at night.

And Paul seems pretty confident about these new Christians being ready for the return of Jesus on the day of the Lord, whenever that day turns out to be, because, unlike the thief in the night, they are no longer going about their business—living their lives—in darkness—the darkness of the world—the darkness of sin.

---

[217] Mark 13:32.
[218] Matthew 24:42-43.

Listen to what Paul is saying. The difference between being a Christian and not being a Christian is the difference between night and day—or, if you wish, between darkness and light.

And what kind of difference is that?

Let's go back to Genesis 1, and the first moment of Creation:

"In the beginning, God created the heavens and the earth. The earth was without form and void, and darkness was over the face of the deep. And the Spirit of God was hovering over the face of the waters.

"And God said, 'Let there be light,' and there was light. And God saw that the light was good. And God separated the light from the darkness. God called the light Day, and the darkness he called Night. And there was evening and there was morning, the first day."[219]

ॐ

Light and darkness—day and night—are about as different as you can get—as different as God can make them, except that God didn't make darkness. God only made light. Darkness was the nothing that was there before God came to the nothing and caused something—something good and God-like: light.

God created light and called it "day." This was the first "day of the Lord." And since that day, at the command of God, the light has alternated with the darkness, just as night gives way to day.

But the Bible teaches that just as the world began with a day of the Lord, it will end with one as well.[220] Centuries before the coming of Christ, the people of God were already looking forward to that day—longing for it—and for the deliverance it would bring from all the darkness of their lives.[221] Life had become too much like the darkness. Interestingly enough, given the choice, people tended to identify with the darkness a lot more often than the light.[222] And they still do.

---

[219] Genesis 1:1-5, ESV.
[220] Acts 2:20; 1 Corinthians 1:8; 2 Peter 3:10.
[221] Ezekiel 30:3; Amos 5:18.
[222] Isaiah 5:20.

Paul calls this "belonging to the night" or "to the darkness." Because of sin, this is the basic condition of all of us. Look around you and see all the ways that people choose darkness rather than light. See how our culture, our society, our public and private institutions have celebrated darkness and rejected light. Given the option of life or death, many choose death. Given the choice of good or bad, many embrace the bad, gladly, and enthusiastically call it "good." See how often immorality is promoted and traditional, biblical morality is ignored, ridiculed and repudiated. The easy evil wins out over the difficult good.

Why is this so?

Those who like the darkness like it because they and their actions cannot be seen as they would be in the light of day. Whether they sleep the night away in moral indifference, inattentive to spiritual things, or use the darkness as a cloak behind which they intoxicate themselves with attitudes and behaviors that distract them from God and impair their ability to meet God's demands upon their lives, they have chosen darkness rather than light. They are what Paul calls "children of the night." Darkness becomes the basic characteristic of their identity.

Finally, in our day, these people proclaim with arrogance their liberty from the constraints of traditional values. They distain time-tested and well-established social virtues.

They revel in their self-assigned freedom to indulge every selfish and irresponsible impulse, oblivious to the impact of their actions on the lives of their victims, the social fabric of their communities or the forbearance of a righteous God.

☙❧

But there is a problem.

The darkness that obscures their sinful lives from the scrutiny of others also obscures their vision of things pertaining to the light. The children of the night, by choosing darkness, come to belong to the darkness. And in that darkness, they will be unable to see, or prepare themselves for, the coming day of the Lord. On that coming day of the Lord, when Jesus Christ, the Light of the world, returns, the separation of darkness from light that first began in Creation will be made complete and final.

For the children of light, the darkness of sin and suffering will go away as they enter an eternity of light. But the opposite is also true. Heaven, you see, is all light and no darkness. Hell, on the other hand, is all darkness and no light.

When the Son of God returns, He will gather the children of darkness and say, for them, "Let there be *no* light!" And there will be no light—none—ever again.[223] And as the children of the day have prepared themselves for His coming, ready and alert at all times because they did not know in advance the exact time it was to be, so from that day on, the children of darkness will be forever alert—but to no avail. Theirs will be an eternity of suffering they will never be able to see coming, because there will never be any light in the world-without-God to which they go.

For the children of the night, the children of darkness, on the day of the Lord's coming, the light will go away—forever. For all eternity, there will be only darkness—complete and total darkness. It will be—hell.

I've tried to imagine hell. I'm reminded of being inside a ship when it loses power at sea. The ship is "dead in the water." Everything shuts down. The propellers stop turning. There is no electricity to run the air conditioning, the lights or any of the countless machines located throughout the vessel. In Navy parlance, we go "hot, dark, and quiet."

If Jesus and Paul are to be believed, two-thirds of that description accurately (if inadequately) describe hell. Hell will be unbearably hot and absolutely dark.

But it will not be quiet.

---

[223] Matthew 25:30-33, 41.

The sound of billions of voices continuously wailing in agony will be so loud that no one person will be able to discern his own cries from all the others.[224]

⇛⇝

"But *you*," Paul says emphatically, *"are not in darkness that this day should surprise you like a thief."* "You are all children of the light and children of the day."

We (thank God!) do not belong to the night or the darkness. We belong to the day. All of us Christians—the new ones, and the old ones—great Christians like Paul and "barely" Christians like…well…most of us—all of us are children of the light. We belong to the day—the great and glorious day of the Lord and His coming.

How come?

Well, in the words of Isaiah's prophesy, *"The people living in darkness have seen a great light."*[225]

Jesus put it this way: *"I am the light of the world. Whoever follows me will never walk in darkness, but will have the light of life."*[226]

"Put your trust in the Light while you have it, so that you may become children of Light. I have come into the world as a Light, so that no one who believes in Me should stay in darkness."

Paul tells the Thessalonian converts, *"Our Lord Jesus Christ…died for us so that…we may live together with him."*

"For God did not appoint us to suffer wrath" (as the children of darkness will on the day Jesus returns), God appointed us to receive salvation through what Jesus did. By our conversion to Christ, we who were children of darkness are made children of the day.

⇛⇝

---

[224] Matthew 8:12; 13:41-42.
[225] Isaiah 9:2, RSV.
[226] John 8:12, ESV.

Think about what that means. This is your essential character as a believer. Because of Christ, you walk in the light. But it's more than that. You belong to the day; you are of it and you will be a participant in all the good that will happen on that day of the Lord's return.

Because you believe in Christ, you live your life with Christ and you expect His return and know that it will be like what you are already experiencing in your relationship with Christ—only more and better.

When Jesus comes back, will you be surprised, since you don't know the time or date?

For children of the day, who live always prepared for His return, the surprise will be like a surprise party you know is planned. You know it will happen someday, so that when the light goes on and all the children of light at the party yell "Surprise!" all you will experience is the in-breaking of joy as you realize the waiting is over, and that it was more than worth the wait, and that you are more than glad you were ready.

So how does a child of the day get and stay ready for the day of the Lord?

Paul says, "Put on the Christian's armor of faith, love and hope to protect yourself from the dangerous things in the darkness, the evil things that come at you out of the night.[227]

There's a bumper sticker I see around from time to time. It says, "Jesus is coming back. Look busy."

Leaving the irreverence aside, Jesus is coming back, but more important than *how* you look when He returns is that you *are looking* for His return, and living in ready anticipation of that day, as children of the light—children of the day. We don't know when our Lord is coming back, but we do know when we need to be ready for His return: now and always. Amen.

৯৯৯

---

[227] Ephesians 6:10-17.

27.

In All Circumstances

1 Thessalonians 5:18 RSV

...give thanks in all circumstances; for this is the will of God in Christ Jesus for you.

కొంⱪ

Several weeks ago, I participated in the annual fundraiser we hold for the nation's candy makers. Every year, loyal, patriotic Americans flock to their local grocery stores by the millions to clear the shelves of chocolate bars and lollipops (at no small expense) and turn them over to millions of diminutive junk food disposal experts who appear with the setting of the sun to ring doorbells or reach into opened trunks in church parking lots and relieve the goodie purchasers of their burdens.

Though this colossal transfer of caloric treasure is probably the closest thing to an empirical proof of the existence of heaven in the pre-adolescent mind, their joy and excitement do not automatically lead to expressions of gratitude. In the shadows behind almost every costumed collector is an adult prompting: "What do you say?"

(One enterprising connoisseur at my door responded, "Can I have another Kit-Kat?")

The correct answer, as it turns out, is "Thank you." And with persistent prompting, most of the ghosts and goblins, pirates and princesses were able to parrot the words with various degrees of enthusiasm.

My point in describing this ritual is to suggest to you that giving thanks is not a natural activity for most human beings. Responsible adults remind their children to say, "thank you," in the hope that the habit, if frequently reinforced, will "stick."

Responsible adults like Moses and David, Nehemiah and Ezra were constantly prompting the children of Israel to give thanks to God. Throughout the Old Testament, God's people are told,

> *"O, give thanks unto the Lord for he is good;*
> *his steadfast love endures forever."*[228]

Of course, if everybody were giving thanks, the Bible writers probably wouldn't have needed to say anything to them about doing so.

In the New Testament, Paul does a bit of prompting of his own. In the fifth chapter of his first letter to the Thessalonians, he writes: *"Give thanks in all circumstances, for this is the will of God in Christ Jesus for you."* And since we are participating this week in the annual fundraiser we hold for the nation's turkey raisers and cranberry growers, I will parrot the words of Saint Pail to you: *"Give thanks…."*

And that concludes the sermon for today.

శంఖ

…or would, except that Paul says more than *"Give thanks."* Paul says, *"Give thanks—**in all circumstances**."*

Why *"in all circumstances"*?

C. S. Lewis says, "We ought to give thanks for all fortune: if it is "good," because it is good; if it is "bad," because it works in us

---

[228] 1 Chronicles 16:34; Psalm106:7; Jeremiah 33:11.

patience, humility, and the contempt of this world and the hope of our eternal country."[229]

Is this just a gimmick to make us feel better when disappointment or even disaster makes us feel bad—or worse? Sort of like the old saying: "Well, praise the Lord, anyway"?

There are a lot of circumstances that don't bring gratitude readily to mind. A lot of people have lost their homes in Southern California in recent weeks. Others are losing life or limb in Iraq and Afghanistan. I bet all of those folks don't feel much like giving thanks. Just about everybody feels like singing the words from that old spiritual: "Nobody knows the trouble I've seen…"—if not now, then sometime.

But Paul doesn't say, "Give thanks when you feel like it—when the circumstances are favorable, and everything is working out all right." He says, *"Give thanks in all circumstances."*

We celebrate out Thanksgiving holiday in remembrance of the Pilgrims, or the Jamestown settlers, or "whoever" who came to this country and quickly started dying of disease, starvation, and hostile encounters with local peoples. They gathered, in a formal way, to give thanks, as much for the many bad things that didn't happen to them, as for the few good things that did.

But giving thanks in all circumstances is not a psychological gimmick. Paul does not say, "Give thanks *for* all things." He says, "Give thanks *in* all things." Not everything is worthy of gratitude. Not every situation is a good thing. But gratitude *in* every situation is different from gratitude *for* every situation.

So why does Paul say, "Be grateful in every circumstance"?

Because he also says in Romans 8:28, *"We know that—in everything—God works—for good—with those who love him—who are called according to his purpose."*[230]

---

[229] C.S. Lewis, *The Quotable Lewis*, Wayne Martindale and Jerry Root, eds. London: Tyndale, 1990, p. 579.
[230] Romans 8:28, RSV.

What is it about *"in all circumstances"* that is worthy of our gratitude?

If you do not see a reason to give thanks in your circumstances, look harder; it's there. Look at your life when it's difficult. Where do you think God is? When the Hebrews thought they were trapped between a mighty sea and a mighty army, God parted the waters for them, and then washed their enemies away.[231] When God's people thought they would starve in the desert, God dropped food out of heaven.[232]

When the storm raged in the lives of the disciples, Jesus made the winds be still.[233] When they thought Jesus was dead and gone forever, He appeared among them and gave them the strength and courage and wisdom to survive.[234] We are to give thanks in every situation because God is in every situation. In every situation, God is either providing the blessing or redeeming the sorrow.

Gratitude in all things requires a different perspective—a deeper, more spiritual understanding. Gratitude in all things requires discernment—seeing the meaning of things as God defines them. Can you believe that one day you will feel like giving God thanks for everything? One day, you will be able to see how God redeemed every disappointment—every pain—every loss.

Look back over your life. Is there not something that you wanted desperately, and now say, "Thank God I didn't get my way about that!" Is there not something you dreaded, that now you see as the source of some great blessing? "If that hadn't happened, I never would have—or could have—grown or gained that other blessing."

Is there some grief in your heart that lingers and festers and leaves you anything but grateful? If you cannot yet see God's redemption of it, you will.

---

[231] Exodus 14:10-31.
[232] Exodus 16:2-15.
[233] Mark 4:36-41.
[234] John 20:19-20.

And because you will, Paul says give thanks in advance for what you know is coming. Give thanks and begin to experience release—deliverance—from what otherwise hardens your heart and holds you captive in the spirit of ingratitude.

The Swiss theologian Karl Barth said that "basically…all sin is ingratitude."[235] When Paul describes the character of ungodly, wicked men in the first chapter of Romans, he says, *"although they knew God, they did not honor him as God—or give thanks to him."*[236]

Give thanks in all circumstances because God is in all circumstances, working for good with those who love Him and are called according to His purpose. That's very good news and I'm glad I can share it with you this morning.

ॐ•ॐ

Now, at this point, I need to quote to you those great words repeated in countless late-night commercials: "But wait! There's more!"

Paul says that giving thanks in all circumstances *"is the will of God—in Christ Jesus—for you."* I think this verse is kind of like an algebra problem. Remember algebra? Algebra is that math you didn't understand in school, but had to study, because you would never use it again after you left school. Well, now it turns out that I need a little algebra to interpret the Bible and preach this sermon. Who knew!?

Anyway, algebra says that if you find two equal parts on the opposite sides of an equation, you can subtract them both without changing the equation. There are two phrases in this verse that begin with the preposition "in": "in all circumstances" and "in Christ Jesus." What I have been saying so far is that, for the Christian," these two phrases are equal: The Christian is in Christ

---

235 Karl Barth, "The Doctrine of Reconciliation: The Subject-Matter and Problems of the Doctrine of Reconciliation," *Church Dogmatics, Volume 4/1*, New York, NY: A&C Black, 2004, pp. 41-42.
236 Romans 1:21, RSV.

Jesus in all circumstances. If you remove those two phrases, the "biblical" equation become simpler: giving thanks "equals" the will of God for you.

A lot of people want to know what the will of God is for them. They do a lot of things to try to find out what it is. The Bible offers a few insights. First Thessalonians 4:3 says, *"It is God's will that you should be sanctified."*[237] First Peter 2:15 says, *"It is God's will that by doing good you should silence the ignorant talk of foolish people."*[238]

Jesus tells the disciples in Matthew that *"it is not the will of your Father who is in heaven that one of these little ones should perish."*[239] And 1st Thessalonians 5:18 says, *"Give thanks...for it is the will of God—for you."*

Have you ever thought that God is the only One Who has no need to be grateful? There is nothing that God needs that He cannot provide for Himself. In fact, there is nothing that God needs—period. There is nothing that God wants that He could not provide all by Himself if He wanted to. That's what it means to be "the Creator of the universe."

So, if there is something God wants—like faith or trust or obedience—or gratitude—that He chooses not to cause to be, it must be because there is a reason is should come to Him freely—without coercion. It is not any benefit these things would provide to Himself that God seeks. So, it must be the benefit that comes to those who *offer* these things—freely. What do you suppose the benefit is to us of our experience and expression of gratitude?

John Piper says that "gratitude to God is a response to being cared for by a great God. It signifies that God is the Source of our safety and meaning in life. It's the mark of a secure, healthy, mature person."[240]

---

[237] 1 Thessalonians 4:3, NIV.

[238] 1 Peter 2:15, NIV.

[239] Matthew 18:14, RSV.

[240] John Piper, "Prison Profanity and the Meaning of Advent," *Desiring God* blog, December 4, 1989.

Maybe that's why our giving thanks is God's will for us. It would be just like a God Whose *"steadfast love endures forever."*[241]

৵৵৹

Many people will be on the road this week, making their way home for Thanksgiving. They're going home to be with family. They're going home for a feast that will go on and on. All the time they're going, they will know where they're going and what awaits them.

Suppose there are some steep hills along their way. Are they going to be any less excited about going home? Suppose they hit a few potholes or encounter a detour or two. Suppose the car breaks down or the traffic backs up.

Will they give up? Will they stop wanting to go home—stop caring about getting home for Thanksgiving?

Or will the desire to get home, and the knowledge of all the joy that awaits them, restore their hope and sustain their determination to go on?

Whatever the circumstances, they're going to be thinking about Thanksgiving. And whatever the circumstances, Thanksgiving will keep them going.

Whatever the circumstances, Thanksgiving will keep us going, too.

Give thanks with a grateful heart.[242] *"Give thanks in all circumstances, for this is the will of God in Christ Jesus for you."*

৵৵৹

---

[241] Psalm 100:5.
[242] Henry Smith, "Give Thanks with a Grateful Heart," 1978.

From the First Letter to Timothy

1 Timothy 1:12-17 ESV

[12] I thank him who has given me strength, Christ Jesus our Lord, because he judged me faithful, appointing me to his service, [13] though formerly I was a blasphemer, persecutor, and insolent opponent. But I received mercy because I had acted ignorantly in unbelief, [14] and the grace of our Lord overflowed for me with the faith and love that are in Christ Jesus. [15] The saying is trustworthy and deserving of full acceptance, that Christ Jesus came into the world to save sinners, of whom I am the foremost. [16] But I received mercy for this reason, that in me, as the foremost, Jesus Christ might display his perfect patience as an example to those who were to believe in him for eternal life. [17] To the King of the ages, immortal, invisible, the only God, be honor and glory forever and ever. Amen.

⇛‹

John 21:14-17 ESV

[14] This was now the third time that Jesus was revealed to the disciples after he was raised from the dead.

[15] When they had finished breakfast, Jesus said to Simon Peter, "Simon, son of John, do you love me more than these?" He said to him, "Yes, Lord; you know that I love you." He said to him, "Feed my lambs." [16] He said to him a second time, "Simon, son of John, do you love me?" He said to him, "Yes, Lord; you know that I love you." He said to him, "Tend my sheep." [17] He said to him the third time, "Simon, son of John, do you love me?" Peter was grieved because he said to him the third time, "Do you love me?" and he said to him, "Lord, you know everything; you know that I love you." Jesus said to him, "Feed my sheep."

⇛‹

28.

Why Mercy?

1 Timothy 1:12-17; John 21:14-17 ESV

In a few moments, you will get up out of your seat, make you way to the center aisle, and, when your turn comes, take your place at the table of your Lord.

What do you think about as the elements of communion are prepared and the process is explained? What floats through your mind—what do you *bring* to mind—as you wait—as you step forward—as you hold out your hand for the sacred bread to be placed there?

Let me give you something to think about today—a point to ponder. You can start now.

Consider these four words: *"But I received mercy."*

The Apostle Paul writes these four words to his younger friend and colleague, Timothy, in the passage you heard this morning. This is a Paul who is nearing the end of his life and his ministry on this earth. In his three letters to Timothy and Titus (another of his longtime helpers), Paul is turning over leadership in churches he founded to the next generation and giving advice for guiding an ever-growing Church.

And in the midst of it all, Paul takes a moment to reflect in wonder on his remarkable life.

And among the most amazing things about his amazing life—to him—is not all the places he has been or the people he has met or even the impact he has had. It is this: He received mercy.

This is an amazing, marvelous miracle to Paul—even at the end of his life—because Paul has never forgotten who he is—and who he had been. He mentions it twice.

The *"I received mercy"* is prefaced, both times, with the word *"but."* Mercy is not what he should logically have expected to receive. Even after decades of dedicated service to the cause of Christ, Paul has not forgotten that, before that, he had been a blasphemer, criticizing and cursing Jesus—a persecutor, going after Christians to torture and kill them—and an insolent opponent of Christ and His Church, someone who took a perverted pleasure in the vicious things he was doing to the followers of Christ.

But, despite all that, Paul received mercy.

∂∾∾∾

Yes, that was then—but the second time he talks about receiving mercy, Paul tells Timothy, "I am the foremost of sinners." Not "I was," but "I *am*"—present tense. Paul knows himself still—at the end of his life— as the foremost of sinners. The only difference now is that, one day years before, Paul received mercy from Jesus Christ.

Listen to what he's saying: "Even insolent opponents of Christ can receive mercy and be converted—even 'super sinners' can receive mercy and serve the Lord faithfully and effectively." To paraphrase a recent movie title: "Mercy is for Real!"[243]

But why? Why would—why does—God have mercy on people who have spent their lives doing everything they can to oppose Him and offend Him—and plan to go on doing more of the same every chance they get?

---

[243] The movie in question is *Heaven is for Real*, a 2014 film about a four-year-old boy who experiences heaven during emergency surgery.

That's an interesting question and we could have a long and lively discussion about it. But there's a better, more important question: "Why would—why does—God have mercy—on you?"

And if you're at a loss for answers, Paul has a couple that might prove useful. Paul says, *"I received mercy because I had acted ignorantly in unbelief."*

But Paul was a Bible scholar; he was "into" his religion—hook, line and sinker. But when what you believe is the wrong thing, and you believe it passionately, it means you're not going to believe the right thing, passionately or otherwise. Your wrong belief is unbelief as far as God is concerned. And if that is true, everything you think is going to be ignorance rather than wisdom. You're in a downward, unbreakable cycle, a death spiral—unless God intervenes—with mercy.

And that's why—like Paul—you received mercy: you *had* to—and God knew it.

And the good news about your receiving God's mercy is that with it—if you accept it—you also receive His overflowing grace that enables you to respond to Him with genuine faith and love instead of hatred and hostility.

Why mercy?

Because the God and Father of our Lord Jesus Christ wants you to be more than a rebel He must punish. He wants you to be the loving, obedient child He created you to be—and without His mercy, you can't be.

❧

But Paul puts his finger on another reason for God's mercy: *"I received mercy,"* he tells Timothy, *"so that in me, as the foremost sinner, Jesus Christ might display his perfect patience as an example...."*

The mercy God has shown you shows other people that God is a God Who shows mercy—and will—even to them. You are the example—the proof—to everyone who sees you—that mercy is available and may be received.

So don't be pretending that you didn't receive God's mercy—or that you didn't need it—or you'll mess up one of God's primary reasons for showing you mercy in the first place.

❧

In the middle of this passage, Paul quotes a line that must have been familiar in the early church. It's familiar to the folks in our early service because we quote it every Sunday ourselves: *"Christ Jesus came into the world to save sinners."*

Sinners are the only kind of people Jesus came into the world to save. The rest, I guess, are on their own. And to be saved, every sinner has got to receive the mercy God gives through Jesus Christ. And, again, the only people who can receive this mercy are sinners. So that's why you and I and Paul received mercy.

❧

In a few moments, you will get up out of your seat, make you way to the center aisle, and, when your turn comes, you will take your place at the table of your Lord. And you will think: "Wow! I received mercy."

In fact, that's why you can come and stand at this table. That's why there is—and always will be—a place here for you. That's why, even after you receive the bread and the wine—even after you put your arms around those sinners on either side of you[244]—even after you pray and go your way back to your seat, you will continue to be the recipient of that divine, undeserved mercy, wondering how God could love you so much, and witnessing to the world that He does.

❧

---

[244] It was the practice at our church during communion for participants to gather around a tall table to receive the elements, and then to embrace each other in something of a "huddle" as the minister prayed over the group before they returned to their seats.

Now let me squeeze just a little more out of this passage of scripture and we'll be done.

Paul responds to the realization that he has received God's amazing, unmerited mercy in two ways. They form the bookends of what he writes Timothy in this paragraph—the opening verse and the closing verse.

Paul begins, *"I thank him…"*

Who?

"Christ Jesus our Lord."

For what?

For giving Paul the strength to be the proof that a sinner—any sinner—every sinner—the worst sinner—can receive God's mercy.

For judging Paul faithful in the years since he received mercy rather than judging him guilty because he needed mercy so badly in the first place.

For putting Paul in the place of honor in the front line of the fight against evil and the kind of life that Paul had once lived.

When you have received God's mercy, you come to Him in gratitude—and you give Him—for the gift of mercy—praise. Paul pens his own doxology—or again—he recalls one for Timothy that they would have shared many times with many other Christians in worship:

> *"To the King of the ages,*
> *immortal, invisible, the only God,*
> *be honor and glory*
> *forever and ever. Amen."*

❧

You have received mercy—and now you know why.

Praise and thanksgiving—honor and glory—to our God and King forever—and today at His table.

Amen.

❧

From the Second Letter to Timothy

2 Timothy 1:1-14 ESV

¹ *Paul, an apostle of Christ Jesus by the will of God according to the promise of the life that is in Christ Jesus,*

² *To Timothy, my beloved child:*

Grace, mercy, and peace from God the Father and Christ Jesus our Lord.

³ *I thank God whom I serve, as did my ancestors, with a clear conscience, as I remember you constantly in my prayers night and day.* ⁴ *As I remember your tears, I long to see you, that I may be filled with joy.* ⁵ *I am reminded of your sincere faith, a faith that dwelt first in your grandmother Lois and your mother Eunice and now, I am sure, dwells in you as well.* ⁶ *For this reason I remind you to fan into flame the gift of God, which is in you through the laying on of my hands,* ⁷ *for God gave us a spirit not of fear but of power and love and self-control.*

⁸ *Therefore do not be ashamed of the testimony about our Lord, nor of me his prisoner, but share in suffering for the gospel by the power of God,* ⁹ *who saved us and called us to a holy calling, not because of our works but because of his own purpose and grace, which he gave us in Christ Jesus before the ages began,* ¹⁰ *and which now has been manifested through the appearing of our Savior Christ Jesus, who abolished death and brought life and immortality to light through the gospel,* ¹¹ *for which I was appointed a preacher and apostle and teacher,* ¹² *which is why I suffer as I do. But I am not ashamed, for I know whom I have believed, and I am convinced that he is able to guard until that day what has been entrusted to me.* ¹³ *Follow the pattern of the sound words that you have heard from me, in the faith and love that are in Christ Jesus.*

¹⁴ *By the Holy Spirit who dwells within us, guard the good deposit entrusted to you.*

᠍ᢋᢀᡧ

29.

The Future of the Species

2 Timothy 1:1-14 ESV

Every living thing is designed to reproduce itself. When a life form does not do so, it soon ceases to exist. If you watch any of the popular nature programs—documentaries about animals or plants—you will hear a continuous litany of dire warnings about the uncertain future of this species or that: its congenial climate is changing—its natural habitat is shrinking—vicious predators are taking their toll—its chances of survival are grim.

There is a particular species that has become a popular subject of such dire warning—in documentaries and elsewhere. The climate has become less conducive to it of late and many of the locations where it has traditionally thrived don't see nearly the number of individual specimens as they once did. In some of those areas, the species is virtually extinct, and in other traditional habitats, it faces an increase in attacks from both long-time enemies and new foes as well.

But for this particular species, negative trends in environment have generally had little impact on long-term viability. Adversity has, historically, stimulated growth, both individually and collectively.

In areas where the species once flourished but now appears extinct—and even in areas where the species once thrived but now is struggling—the basis for this downturn in potential health and vitality appears to be attributable to one unusual factor: vast numbers of the species show neither effort nor inclination to reproduce themselves. Specimens that seem, to all outward appearances, to be perfectly healthy and fully functional rarely replicate themselves. Countless specimens will never, across the full course of their existence on earth, attempt to cause another example of their species to come into being.

As I indicated, increasingly adverse environmental conditions do not seem to be the challenge diminishing the species. The vast majority of this species eat well and engage in a wide assortment of activities. In fact, they engage in a broader range of activities than they ever did before. The species just will not reproduce, as a rule.

The species does not seem to have gone through a mutation that would make replication impossible. This conclusion is based on the well-documented, though rare, examples of very prolific reproduction by specimens of the species that seem to have no new or unique capability. In those cases, there is no indication that "setting" is a factor, either.

Nor is there a set process discerned to guarantee success. It just seems that those who attempt to reproduce succeed to some degree, whatever they do, while those that never make the effort, never account for the birth of another representative of the species.

The endangered branch of the species may not have mutated, but the reproductive impetus does seem to have migrated, generally south and east.

It has gone so far south and east that it has jumped whole continents and set off a remarkable resurgence of the species in places not historically associated with it.

As a whole, the species is thriving. You can take it off the endangered list, and keep it off, as long as there are significant numbers of specimens who do not allow themselves to be hampered, restricted or otherwise prevented from reproducing the species as they are all intended to do. No external influence can limit the success of this basic operation.

And if the resurgence of the species in unusual and faraway places continues, the seemingly inconceivable could happen: the dwindling number of specimens in traditional locations could experience a resurgence. The strength, number and impact on other species could be reversed, all because the specimens located in the danger zones decided to commit themselves to the reproduction of their kind.

And what is this odd species—this life form—with so many specimens that will not do what all living things are designed to do—that simply choose not to replicate themselves?

Why, I thought you knew.

It's called "the modern Christian."

৯০৬

30.

Remember Jesus Christ

2 Timothy 2:8 RSV

Remember Jesus Christ, raised from the dead, descended from David, as preached in my gospel….

ॐ

"Remember Jesus Christ."

What an odd thing for the great Apostle Paul to say to his faithful and beloved protégé, Timothy. Here's a young fellow out on the front lines of the fight, giving his all for the cause, and the best Paul can come up with is, *"Remember Jesus Christ"*?

Timothy has given his life to Jesus Christ. He is serving Jesus every day. A lot of the difficulties Timothy is encountering are the result of his being associated with this new Jesus movement. How about coming up with "The 7 Habits of Highly Effective Mission Pastors"?[245]

Well, Paul has given Timothy a lot of good, practical advice like that in the two letters addressed to the young man, but at this point, Paul simply says, *"Remember Jesus Christ."* It's not the first time a disciple has been reminded to remember. Jesus Himself told

---

[245] To paraphrase Stephen Covey's *The 7 Habits of Highly Effective People*, New York, NY: Simon and Schuster, 1989.

His followers to remember His words to them[246] and He scolded them in their anxiety for not remembering that He had fed five thousand people with a few loaves of bread.[247] The real surprise is not that a committed Christian would be reminded to remember Christ, but that he or she would need to be reminded so often.

We get so distracted by the details of our Christian duties—so disturbed by the difficulties that crowd around us as Christians in this sad and sinful world—that we constantly engage the world without the awareness of the One Who first engaged us with His love and grace and power. We see the circumstances that need attention and lose sight of Jesus Christ, Who is what every circumstance needs.

⊱⋅⊰

So, this morning, at this moment, you be Timothy. Forget everything else—and remember Jesus Christ. Remember Who He is. Remember what He has done for you. Remember what He has said to you. Remember how He feels about you. Remember what He is doing for you right now—and will continue to do for you for all eternity.

Remember, as Paul says, that Jesus Christ—your Jesus Christ—has been *"raised from the dead."* You are not merely recalling a historical figure—long dead and gone. You are renewing an ongoing relationship, drawing upon the infinite reservoir of encouragement, wisdom and power Jesus possesses and provides. He is your Savior, your Friend, your Support, your Strength, your Guide—in every circumstance —every moment—every day—forever.

So remember Jesus Christ—*"raised from the dead."* And remember, also, that He is—to put it in a nutshell— *"descended from David."*

What does that mean?

---

[246] John 16:4.
[247] Matthew 16:9.

Jesus Christ—your Jesus Christ—is the fulfillment of every promise God ever made to His people.[248] He is God's timeless plan for replacing sin with salvation.[249] He is the culmination of every sacred law and every prophetic utterance.[250] He is the purpose for every act of God in nature and nations and individual human hearts.[251] Remember Jesus Christ—Who He was—Who He is—and Who He will always be.

When you are suffering like a soldier on the battlefield of sickness or conflict—remember Jesus Christ. When you are striving to achieve some goal in the arena of moral endeavor—remember Jesus Christ. When you are toiling in the field of duty and service to sow the seeds for a Christian harvest—remember Jesus Christ. Remember Jesus Christ and He will protect you and strengthen you and preserve you.

❧

Remember Jesus Christ—for He remembers you. That's why a thief on a cross would cry out, *"Jesus, remember me!"* And why Jesus would reply, *"...this day you will be with me in Paradise."*[252] That's why Jesus Christ would gather His disciples in an upper room and give them bread and wine to eat and drink and tell them, *"Do this in remembrance of me."*[253]

Do not be distracted, even by your devotion to the work of the kingdom. In the mist of your worst trials and your best efforts, *"remember Jesus Christ."*

❧

---

[248] Luke 1:67-75.
[249] Galatians 4:4-5.
[250] Matthew 5:17.
[251] Colossians 1:16.
[252] Luke 23:42-43, NIV.
[253] Luke 22:19, NIV.

Indices

Sermon Titles in Alphabetical Order

Sermon Titles in Alphabetical Order

Sermon Texts in Biblical Order

Sermon Texts in Biblical Order

Text	Title	Page

Sermon Texts in Lectionary Order

Sermon Texts in Lectionary Order

Related Sermons in Other Volumes

Related Sermons in Other Volumes

Additional Scripture Passages Referenced

Additional Scripture Passages Referenced

Additional Scripture Passages Referenced

Additional Scripture Passages Referenced

Additional Scripture Passages Referenced

Additional Scripture Passages Referenced

Additional Scripture Passages Referenced